Triad Light

Lightbody Awakening
into Triad Relationship

Rosemary Linseman

2012
Published by the Author
Ontario, Canada

Triad Light
Lightbody Awakening into Triad Relationship
3rd revised corrected and expanded edition
first published in paperback 2007,
ebook 2nd edition 2010 with full colour images

Cover Design, Painting and Formatting/Interior Design
by Rosemary Linseman

To order copies of this title, please visit online at:
http://www.createspace.com/3758188
http://www.amazon.com
email: rosemarylinseman@hotmail.com

Library and Archives Canada Cataloguing in Publication

Linseman, Rosemary
    Triad light : lightbody awakening into
triad relationship / Rosemary Linseman.

3rd rev. and corrected ed. of: Twin-light.
ISBN 978-0-9783641-1-3

1. Self-actualization (Psychology)--Poetry.
2. New Age movement. I. Title.

PS8623.I56T94 2012   C811'.6   C2011-904394-7

Dedication...

To my daughter, Meryl
for her unending gestures of Love and wisdom,

to my parents, sparks within my humanity
with their legacy of faith and trust in so much more,

and to our family of All
who have given their light, shining out their truth.

Vie

When I breathe with you

I breathe in a whole, new life

our light and love of life

Contents

Introduction

Through a language of the Soul, poetry and prose inspire as one changes so profoundly through a process of growth into much higher dimensions of consciousness. And it is through this kind of language that I share inspired ideas and feelings about this process affecting changing relationship on every level of existence in our world. We are at a time of a great adjustment or paradigm shift as dimensional consciousness comes together or converges for all as we are adapting through a much higher connection of relationship firstly within ourselves, with others and our Earth through an evolutionary accelerated awakening process that is synchronistic with All who choose greater growth consciously.

We are all linked on many levels, including familiar group-souls or family groups of consciousness and global or mass consciousness but at this time we are growing with more awareness and in ways that are mysteriously much more intertwined through dimensional timelines of synchronistic reoccurances around us in our physical reality. While our relationships with one another and with our Earth have been in an upheaval of chaos for some time, we have reached the point where we are witnessing the collapse in old consciousness of our known and changing world. And what we may have once perceived rationally is not always relevant for us anymore, so that finding answers or searching for some new truth becomes a higher quest, an unravelling of the mystery as we build our bond of trust within developing higher relationship during our greater process of growth occurring with All around us.

Building our greater bond of trust is the paradox of what could be termed, the 'twin trials' of our evolutionary history. The ultimate test of our evolution is upon us and how we incorporate our greater strengths and yet challenge our very human nature or limitation is the final trial of our inner to OverSoul-bond of relationship. The primal, twin or yin/yan energies have teetered in a mostly competitive state, where only rare moments of creation intertwine. But this twin story is finding an end for us all, as we learn to trust and follow our 'love-light' bond with choices for change. At every turn our choice determines the strength of that bond, built with courage and faith in a higher way. It is the Over-bond of love that is incubating and preparing us for a new relationship and order in our world that is bringing this union through higher dimensions of yin/yan blending for a promise of a new world consciousness with new higher relationship. Triad relationship is the combined rebirth of three, shared and built between each twin-Soul of pairs. It comes because we choose love, we choose peace - a higher way.

Physical/emotional/mental/spiritual imbalances within each rise through a new calm with adjustments of our new Lightbody development - a blending or combining of higher aspects for a new birth - from a bond conceived long ago between a great many pairs of OverSouls. It is the combined multidimensional consciousness, that many OverSouls have chosen growth together with us for higher solutions to the ongoing imbalance of energies that have surmounted to this point of a collapse of our past world consciousness. The yin/yan aspect energies have been in a norm of codependance of competitive, separate leanings for too long and are now at a crisis - this turning point for a higher togetherness in a new future Earth reality with a wholeness of multidimensional consciousness.

Triad relationship is bringing harmony, peaceful equilibrium at a time when we need it most. This sacred marriage between OverSoul pairs is now expanding for new relationship for this Earth and with their underSouls here for All. A combined shared dimensional whole in each new Overself consciousness - a blending within each is the significant process that many twin Souls now share - with their developing third OverSoul shared consciousness - Triad relationship, to be completed or born here in a future of new community consciousness in a new Earth of whole dimensional existence. Each cannot help but go together as we experience this joining of pairs in both the higher and eventually here in Our new Earth reality, when we each make choices with Our all.

Where we begin our grand, higher path in 'the now' is always rooted in some past or lifetime pattern of belief system of any dimensional timeline - distant to be sure but cycling around but for our recognition. We can 'step it up' to higher perspectives while 'stepping out' of the games, time and again to find ourselves going through accelerated phases of growth. Moving forward past competitive wranglings keeping us stuck in solar plexus, old power-based control tactics or ego protective stances is to clear issues moving on and up to Overself connected motivations, where true strengths are weighed. Here we discover inner inspiration from understanding arising. Through the greater process with each adaptive phase of accelerated collapse in timeline dimensional consciousness come the upsurges of issues or belief systems brought to our awareness and we find understanding and peace. The great calm of comfort of the Kundalini force carries all our blockages with ongoing cleansings and clearings. Our struggles and conflicts are lifted as we find ourselves initiated to higher levels of consciousness, through the trials.

We learn to find ever more equilibrium on ever higher ground as we more fully embrace our Love-Force bond. And it is the Overlove shared between underSouls and consequently all who choose to grow together multidimensionally. For all who embrace both sides within self of our shared twin existence while learning to trust in a special bond to our greater developing Oneness-of-being as each evolves and adapts to higher ways through phases of blendings of consciousness.

Each phase of growth of this great awakening process begins a collapse through higher dimensions of energies linking timeline patterns of beliefs from deeply rooted unprocessed consciousness as we:

➢ *free our wounded/inner-child as barriers of old patterns are revealed with our great nurturer;*

➢ *rediscover our Entirety as we emerge with our greater developing Over connection to our OverSoul;*

➢ *merge with our OverSoul pair bond for higher conscious choices - rebalancing/blending twin aspects of experience;*

➢ *forge our greater bond standing with higher choices; see ego-walls collapse for new beginnings for OverSoul pairs;*

➢ *incorporate more fully Our multidimensional strengths; unlinking root issues to redefine and discover greater roles;*

➢ *focus shifting from both energies, we open and redirect Our specialities or blended dimensional, creative endeavours.*

Most significantly, we discover our intrinsic connection or symbiotic conscious relationship to all of Earth dimension of reality and our challenge to evolve takes on a greater purpose. Our ability to adapt with each phase is an adjustment of the inner-balance and blending of the twin or yin/yan dimensional aspect energies of experience and with the momentum of the once dormant Kundalini force for our Overself evolution. As we make our most important choices for higher conscious living, comfort and requirements arrive along with Our Over-loving upliftment. The evolutionary time of Lightbody consciousness has arrived as we awaken and rise with the dawn of the Triads' Light. We share with All the hope and promise of this grand new age. The birth of Triad relationship of twin Souls of pairs in a new Earth multidimensional reality brings in the new paradigm consciousness - bringing solutions and upliftment to ever higher frequencies of love, bliss harmony and joy.

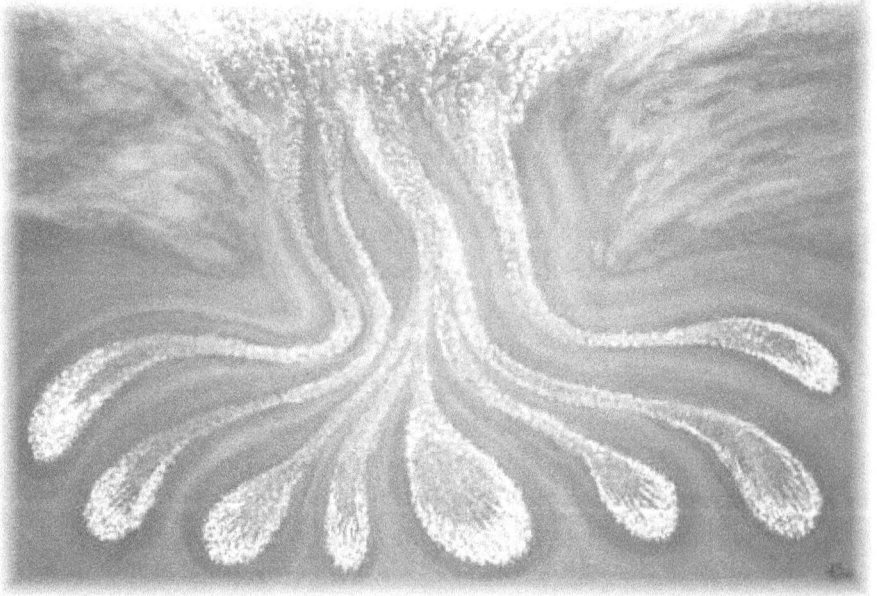

'Earthly Vortex' *(Acrylic, 12"h x 17"w)*

Higher Manifestation: Beginning

Releasing from competitive, solar-plexus based stances
by centering in the Heart with our higher self awareness
and opening to our OverSoul connection

Inward Flight and Expansion

Seeking and Unfoldment

*Free our wounded/inner-child as barriers of old patterns
are revealed with our great nurturer*

Celebrate

All my life
pushed away people
who truly care about me and love me
settle for people who feel less than this
too important, too risky, too painful

Afraid of failure...
expect perfection?
why not expect this
because I look for this outside myself
and not within myself
someone else must live up to my expectations
but they are so high
nobody can possibly fill these
so settle for less
why are they so high
unrealistic?
or is it that I believe they are too high for me

I deserve to celebrate
and fall in Love with the BeLoved
my OverSoul
who is my perfection

Perfect is...
how high you will look
beyond sight
so simple

Your OverSoul wishes all for you - to awaken to a truer identity or higher perspective of the Self and begins with you moving forward courageously into a new understanding of life.

We only 'settle' after we have lost all faith and trust in something so much more for this life - a higher love and respect for oneself as we grow mutually into higher relationship in our world and in synchronicity, mutually with all significant others.

Root Chakra Meditation

When I'm there
I go deep into the Earth
growing like a root system
spreading into Mother Earth
everything I need is there
I'm tapped into the source
what a powerful source!
how secure I feel
this security warms me, envelopes me
receiving what I need
I will always be nourished
by a plentiful supply!
I feel very safe - I am part of this

Oh Mother
you hold me again
as I curl cradled in your womb
growing and glowing with your love
carry me again to that new born place
to breathe a fresh new breath of life

The practise of meditation takes one to much deeper consciousness, to dwelling places of healing unbeknownst to our changing past world consciousness. What we bring out of these higher experiences is the certainty of our divine connection to our OverSoul - to 'All' that is, was and can or will be in dimensional timelines of consciousness. We need only let ourselves be affected by this greater expanse of Love, to bring back a new understanding of hope.

Just help me to let go enough to feel that Love again - surge forth from within me. I want to feel that greater part of 'us' - I get confused by what it means but I know the power of such love as no other could ever explain. And it is my source and my reason above all. It makes me quiver with shame as it makes me swell with joy overflowing.

New Age

It's not the way we understand
the Universal Force of creation
that is the right way
or in any particular time was wrong
it was always the right way
each evolving Soul's way of perceiving
this All Force - always
tradition is still important
with discipline and ritual
but in our way, a modern way
we have evolved, every step just as important
as the preceding one
so we respect all-ways of the eternal now
to take us into the future

Some have rejected their religion
like generations from other times too
this was their truth
still a meaningful pursuit
still kept with principles and traditions
but we need to understand
tap into this force and our own creative force
to evolve any further, to ever attain Oneness
through and with our OverSoul
the way and the destiny

When we accept that our understanding of the Universal Force of creation cannot be limited to concepts that humanity has intended, we can begin to trust in the continuum of a greater process of unfoldment for all life forms within creation here. We can embrace the potential of our divine part in a much larger picture through and with our greater OverSoul connection and with the limitlessness of the All Force of creation; allowing our own evolutionary accelerated unfoldment to begin for us and to some new level of growth along with all others.

The unity or symbiance of the Universal Force or the All Force within our Earth's planes and with the higher dimensions is unimaginably our greatest communion to life and yet is more of a great mystery - concepts that grow within us and in synchronicity with All as we expand in higher consciousness.

I feel my whole life coming full circle now like there is more meaning to it all. My past having some greater relevance in this lifetime - since before the accelerated evolutionary awakening. Like the awakening is part of a bigger picture that is unfolding for all. I have always felt like the awakening was the beginning of an end, that it was more important than everything else but maybe it is part of the whole too. It has a reason for all we have ever loved, have met and will love.

We may feel separate from all that is unfolding around us at times, but we have a critical role in it all. We have the choice to grow with it and for it - or do we just watch and wait for some next time around? All indication is that we are moving through major change at a relatively accelerated pace than ever known before. Towards what? Doom? Have we really been so oblivious so that we are only just now beginning to awaken as we look a little deeper beyond the surface or apparent situation around this Earth? Or are we all now really trying to play 'catch-up'? Years of procrastination, avoidance or maybe just plain hunger for so much more all the time, seem to have caught up with us.

Or maybe positive growth/change has been seeping into our consciousness all along, even gradually - as many do believe, that there is a greater Force, a Universal unfoldment occurring. Some call it a collapse of our known reality because of the new multidimensional consciousness with our lightbody growth. If the idea of us emerging as some kind of 'super' human race that can tackle any problem and come up with amazing solutions seems unlikely then cynicism or lack of trust in the greater good and choices of mankind has surely got the better of us.

But super may be something we discover if we choose, as many are 'stepping-up' and that means incorporating the dimensional or vibrational shift consciously. We need to make a very deep conscious commitment for positive change/growth in our world and it is easier if one keeps an open mind and Heart, letting that higher love fill you up and in turn build your 'bond of trust' with your highest and best conscious choices and then see your 'view' grow and expand in consciousness.

Heartspace

When I look and feel
this resistance, interference, non-support
with family and friends
I've never felt so alone
in all of life
truly alone - is o.k.
for I know I'm on my way
not trying to conform
or please someone else
by sacrificing my trueself

A great deal I cling to
so I am not so isolated
familiar feelings from some known world
support me...
  does he feel for me
  what I felt for him
  I can't deny this feeling
  it's real to me
just like first love
triggering old concepts still holding me
with all these past layers
of unhealthy emotional burdens
letting go even more confusing
now opening to this Heart connection
so real within
trusting in my greater self to carry me forward
and reclaim strengths of purpose
with the love I need
given away so ungratefully, of my past self worth
not shared, not felt truly by others
attracting only what I have held out for love
but I hold out no more of my old concepts of love
as I continually reidentify with my Over-love

May you cherish
each moment of your longing
for tomorrow
as you uncover the sacred truths of your past

As our Heart awakens to a higher love we surface with our greater self perspective but exposed through layers of our past and lifetimes of hurts (including hereditary, pastlives or any timeline linkage of consciousness) and bring clearer insights through the barriers or scars of old beliefs and patterns. We feel a new freedom as these stifling blockages are lifted from our consciousness as we shift to a higher perspective with our greater awareness. Others in our life may try to grasp the changes with the challenging of old concepts/realities as connections are naturally shifted. We find ourselves seemingly alone but truly ready to be reintroduced to newer concepts of our twin love of lifetimes of experience; allowing us to reclaim our strengths with renewed wonder for a higher love that we feel so strongly within yet healing old concepts of love from our youth and distant pasts. And all still unbelievably close through our rebonding of under twinSoul to twinSoul - and with our developing Overbond of Love.

I have been confused about feeling this profound sense of love stirring within me and told myself that I'm feeling this because I'm lonely and afraid - when really - it comes through so powerfully and reminds me of something so deeply engrained in me - at my Core is a forever Love that evolves always higher.

This love is not mine alone and I can't really define it or contain it - nor do I want to. I know if I just let myself feel it - all areas of my life blossom with hope and newness and change - but this growing love usurps old wounds. I wish I could let go enough to allow it the room to expand past my usual boundaries and scourge the blockages of pain effortlessly in its way.

Inner Work

Trying to talk my withdrawn, hidden
inner child
who is frightened, angry, reclusive
to come out
  "I will always love you
  I will protect you
  let me hold you"
realize I need to start saying the things
to my inner child
that we/inner child never heard/hears
  "you are scared aren't you?
  I know - it's going to be o.k.
  you are strong and creative
  you can find a way to conquer, overcome
  any problem when you put your mind to it
  you are deeply sensitive and compassionate
  you are insightful
  you have helped me
  now it's time for me to help you
  you can trust me
  I know you better than anyone else does
  I love you - unconditionally
  that means all of you
  yes - even the devil in you!
  It's what makes you - special you
  inquisitive - curious to the core
  expressive - in a very artistic way

  You've always been curious about sexual exchange
  long before you could relate
  exposed to hurtful acts by others at so young an age
  just our experience for this or from lifetimes too
  though unfortunate it was, yes!
  self discovery at puberty was then mired
  but the time has finally come to celebrate our creative force
  crippling silence no longer keeps us unable to express
  let's celebrate it together - now!"

Definitions

Giving out - a gift
with no thought or intent of something in return
have I done this? oh yes - I guess
but really and truly from my Heart
a healthy Heart?
has it been healthy enough to do this?
and my return from giving
unknowingly I expected my pain to be eased

Letting go
it has always been easier for me
to run away than let-go
easier in the short term
end up carrying the pain with me anyway
my issue is not giving up though
mine is letting go and therefore
hanging on too long to times of hurts
that I carry
to the detriment of others as well as myself

Hanging on
easier to hang on
than face all the skeletons in my closet
guilt, fear and where these come from
from other times carrying abusive patterns
habitually letting others codependantly victimize
until full of self-doubt, self-loathing, mistrust of others
indecisiveness, confusion, impatience - lack of love
always easier to put my trust, decision making
and loving in another before loving self
let them take the risks, make the mistakes
take control and care of me

To uncover ego-barriers reveals our karmic obligatory sacrifices; regrettable or bad karmic prechoices or pacts made by some higher Souls before coming into this lifetime, to take on patterns for others that are carried over in some cases from lifetimes or timelines of deeply rooted group patterns needing balance. With Lightbody awakening we begin reclaiming our higher hopes and dreams for a path to freedom.

Control Issues

Can I control my life?
and take care of myself and a child
logically I say yes - but how well
can I be good at it and enjoy it
every step of the way
trying to avoid control of it all - before
but always a lurking, uneasy feeling there
telling me - no - promising me that there is more
learning to forgive myself and love myself
ensures my ability to love another and be loved
especially within significant partnership
and which means becoming more aware
of the Oneness of the Universal Force of creation
so I can enjoy my life
care for my own inner child and for my daughter
love others and be loved genuinely
because I am not alone in this
this All powerful force flows through and with OverSoul

How do we start again? Only the child-like way masters this; with our greater loving connection we find the courage of abilities again to secure new strategies or routes to move past old coping mechanisms - that have been habitually patterned around absolutely all rigid controls/barriers but which are our past limitations and now life's obstacles to a higher way. The OverSoul helps guide the child within who intuitively knows how to continually flow with change as we are shown the way to move on with ongoing newer ease of transition through life's challenges for ongoing renewal.

This pain is where I hold back. It is where I let myself get stuck up with patterns everywhere of bitter regret, resentment - but mostly sheer anger at utter complacency. I have seen this all too many times. We carry so much of it and it is too much more than any of us can handle most times. I guess that's when we come to each others' rescue as we are going and growing altogether on higher levels. I still firmly believe that as I face each challenge and move successfully on that I do it with the aid of All.

Karma

Where does all this guilt come from
guilt about marriage
letting families down
debt I owe for friendship
why have I felt that I owe something
to everyone at some point or all the time
is this because I believe I am not worthy
of their expressions of love
that they mustn't really care
they just expect something - in return
that this is normal?

Do I expect something in return
yes, I want them to ease my pain
but it doesn't work
my pain lingers on

We have always had a karma signature to carry like a burden of debt or obligation through many lifetimes and timelines and only able to incarnate here in Earth time reality with a set of prechosen challenges or karmic choices based on predetermined 'blueprints' of lifetimes of standing; to return balance through favours - give or receive. These karmic choices follow us through the lineage of time but not beyond the fire of our Heart connection. We truly begin to make our higher choices as we break our karmic links of attachment or promises/pacts leaving our blueprint unresolved.

We still feel these unhealthy pulls of attachment at the solar plexus while all the patterns from built-up layers through time can become stagnant blockages within the physical. We have a choice to open to our higher Soul growth and cleanse or clear through patterns for all concerned. Our issues can come to light through Heart centre connection of our greater awareness. We are freed from limiting cyclical patterns with new insights as to where issues stem and why. Associations of who we have been carrying old concepts with and for greater understanding to trust that significant others may also receive pertinent understanding with enlightenment; as arises with Our greater overall plan of choice - healing as we expand in consciousness.

Child Memories

I have always felt guilty for what I felt
from other's gestures of caring
and affection for me
I questioned their genuineness
and respect for me
I rejected many real, important, close friendships
from males throughout my life
trust had been lost early on
I rejected my sexuality - my femaleness
my power - my love of myself

I could not look at myself in the mirror
the same way after puberty
I had expectations of how I should look
and therefore be somehow - so I thought
I was tall, full figured - and I hated it
I was absolutely beautiful - and I rejected it
just wanted to fit in
standing out was not easy
always been a good hider
hard for me to hide now
I was being noticed - part of me liked it
most of me was scared to death
of being tested and found out
of not measuring up and fitting in
of how really scared I was
of men - didn't trust their motives
of my sexuality - it only had attracted harm

And then later on in life
my beautiful baby girl
she is a precious gift
a best wish of my Heart
to have such a child
she shares her love for growth
and I am learning a love so real,
so whole with her
that I have forgotten
a greater Overlove and growing awareness
of my inner-child

When a child's perception of truth is denied and all trust in their free spirited world has been broken and lost with the major onset of karmic reenactment of traumatic patterns, their experience for freedom of expression is stifled. The onset of puberty with its time of accelerated growth and new beginning for processing of dimensional specialities of strength will rear and out the cast of confusion, frustration, denial and self-doubt at what should be the natural quickening time of our metamorphosis to reawaken and incorporate our dimensional oneness of being. Boredom and hopelessness might at times suppress our emerging strength of abilities and prevail but our greater Over-Expanse of Love continually lights up the path through our OverHeart connection as we follow through with our abandoned or lost ideals. Our past dreams are recognized with child-like intuitive clarity again. And we will most naturally heal or grow with underlying ideals into maturity for our higher world of consciousness.

I have learned to a greater degree to trust what I feel inside - to trust my intuitive - to believe in something more than what I have experienced in this world or observed. I have learned that one cannot always look outside alone, for answers.

But there is more than this. There is the confusion of so many layers of dimensional synchronistic reoccurances all around from this past and all timelines of beliefs and indoctrines and teachings - not all bad certainly. But we haven't allowed or taken into account change/growth with a new emerging consciousness. The problem is always - clarity! To see clearly the point where old beliefs don't fit into all areas of one's growing perspective.

So we need to listen with an open mind but there is so much change all the time and suffering everywhere! Everyone is searching for answers and looking to others for clues. But really we are all just searching desperately for recognition of ourselves. And everyone has that competitive stance that says, "look at me, notice me, I am somebody but I need you to really help define that for me"; we all seem to know though that in the end we can't keep waiting for approval that really only we can give to ourselves anyway. We are looking for something so much greater - for completion and togetherness within self and each other.

'Emotional Rebirth'   *(Acrylic, 14"h x 15"w)*

Manifesting and Synchronicity

We sometimes get confused as to why synchronistic reoccurances get so frequent at times and so annoying and come from every direction too at times and in so many different ways. But basically it is all about manifesting. They can be like the dangling carrots or illusions (fears because we want them so bad but they have always taunted us and disappointed us) as they wash-out as remnants (of old consciousness) around us - sometimes with others doing something we thought we would be doing. (others' wants we have taken on or picked up subconsciously and manifesting as synchronicities when we are ready to move on consciously higher with the associated issues

But sometimes it is the opposite and we see these remnants as fears of something we have been trying to get away from forever it seems, but they just won't let go. And this can be annoying because the more we avoid the fears/illusions coming at us by running away, jumping through hoops or side-tracking/going around or out of our way - well, the Bigger those fears get. Same with the carrots - the more we follow them, the better they look - again all synchronicities that we totally recognize the further we go until 'Poof', they vanish and we are left in a mess.

Emerging

Committing to the Path of the OverHeart

Rediscover our Entirety as we emerge with our greater developing Over connection to our OverSoul

Evolving Beyond In Time	*Parenting*
Unfoldment	*Beholden*
Oh god, I want to feel	*Leap with the Dream*
You keep the pace with me	*Talking to Higher Self*
Evolution	*Memoirs*

Path to Higher Manifestation: Second Step
Embracing the love that comes; leaning on Our OverSouls' strengths,
We begin to identify *old* fears/illusions as either:
1) taunts/carrots or disappointments - unwanted karmic credits
2) annoying demands or expectations - karmic debts holding on

Evolving Beyond In Time

What was Our Creator's plan about
this fall from grace
part of the process of evolution?
the fall - is this our point of no return
no return to what we were
does evolution mean that we go
from something less to something more
is it always an upward momentum
or do we find ourselves on one pathway
only to have it resume again in 1000 or 10,000 years time
what does this mean - there is no time?
evolution changes our direction
onward and unfolding...

When a flower unfolds it changes form
the bud on the branch with a beauty of its own
transforms with equal beauty to full bloom
then continues as it fades
gives back nourishment to the roots and rests
is the next season of growth any more beautiful
or just different and unique in expression
maybe we don't need to evolve anywhere
to just any future timeline and space reality
with 'just in the nick of time' cyclical tail-race mentality
when we stop or 'rest' in the moment
then maybe We are truly creating at higher levels
with Creation's greater continuum
no longer searching and yearning for tomorrows
just enjoying the now, as we move on higher
with the Creator's rhythm

Looking out into the world with eyes of hope sends us on a truthseeker's quest. With the knowings of Our OverSouls' guidance we bravely step out into a new world with renewed wonder and in this way evoke the wisdom of the seer. We sense a greater, more extraordinary process unfolding and moving us beyond limitations within time, as the blending of Our evolving consciousness unfolds in symbiotic relationship with Earth and its adjustments - for the new harmony of Earth's evolution taking us to a new reality consciousness.

The greatest adjustments of the paradigm shift in dimensional consciousness in the Earth dimensional planes of reality affect all power struggles of adaptation from old cyclical patterns and seasons, of rewards and debts, of expectations and rigid rules that have limited spiritual growth for thousands of years. The layered astral planes of spiritual existence are evolving now with our changing physical plane of reality. And with our slightly dimensionally higher Diva or 'Nature Spirit' realm here in the changing physical Earth reality, all of which, we are all evolving into a higher multidimensional reality.

Altogether we are merging or shifting at an accelerated unfoldment to new world Earth reality at this time of convergence of all dimensional time lines with this paradigm shift. The preparations have all been laid out and unfolding along with our OverSouls' Lightbody growth with all and with our Earth's evolution to new world reality consciousness. Through our connection to the greater continuum, We learn to trust and to bring all that is truly required home here.

It's difficult to fathom that a Soul could have say one hundred lifetimes in Earthplane existence, let alone 12 or even more layers of consciousness across all dimensional timelines in the 3rd dimension alone and which all include past, parallels of the present and any and all future timelines for each lifetime. All this leaving us with conceivably 1200 layers of consciousness converging as we move dimensionally higher at this time. And then there is the twin-match with the other possibly 1200 layers that interplay at the higher levels of consciousness - leaving each Soul with possibly 2400 layers of consciousness to interweave and along with all other twinSouls too?! As we are moving into higher awareness we are interplaying or pooling consciousness with many other pairs of OverSoul layers of consciousness.

Expansion is somewhat a daunting idea but if our brain with 3 new chakrum and a Heart centre with a new chakra above and below are not only ready but initiating to some greater degree with lightbody development - then it's most definitely time we all were moving on consciously with the potential of more than 90% of our once dormant brain capacity to absorb, as we evolve beyond limitation. Heart and Mind are converging, preparing for rebirth along with All who choose to embrace this golden age.

Unfoldment

Oh how do I stop
my life, my linear mode of being
to be with You for more than just
a few moments in my day
my linear mode of being
is my yearning and my searching
to find You
it is all I have ever known
and now You tell me to stop
for You are right here with me
just a Heartbeat away

Maybe we never really fell that far within time
do we push our growth to the limit
with our yearning for something more
when all we really need - is to stop
and enjoy, stop and celebrate
our unique expressions
and remember - who we are
beautiful, powerful and evolving spiritual beings

Honour All-of-creation
celebrate your life joyously with the universe
life is so diverse, so complex
I think our Creator's idea of perfection
is the celebration of that diversity and complexity
and when we do this we are never any closer
as we celebrate our lives
with the continuous commitment
for higher expression of specialities, strengths
we are creating, unfolding and evolving
through and with The All-of-creation

When one feels the profound bond of trust that is our OverHeart connection to our OverSoul triad bond and so to the All of creation, there is a sacred patience born out of this experience. A simple truth of finding Oneself in an altered, ever newly developing and more natural state of peace - nowhere else to search in this completeness.

Oh god, I want to feel
your heartbeat in mine
I want to feel that
synchronicity

You keep the pace with me
even as I redirect every action
to hear You closer to me
and then I am tuned
to life's synchronicities

Keeping pace with life's rhythm is not to outpace the old collapsing karmic or evolutionary 'prescript' but to flow through the accelerated adjustments. Trying to out manoeuvre the adjustments because of perceived 'extinction' is the major challenging factor with these generational timelines of consciousness, that are the limiting karmic, originating mentalities - that we can change! We can support the higher order of the greater evolutionary accelerated process by participating with reverence to join in a larger rewriting and fine-tuning of the process occurring with the purity of our open intentions through our Over connection to the greater continuum. With Our continual practise or commitment of living, We can contribute to the greater 'in time' or right time and place unfoldments filtering down.

The terms psychic reading, channelled reading and mediation through a medium are all very common references to getting help when seeking answers from those who are linking and tapping into higher dimensions of consciousness. But we are beginning to learn how to be our own best mediators - that is to say we are beginning to understand that we can learn to find our own common language of interpretation within ourselves as we learn to link vibrationally or dimensionally higher with our own best Source - our OverSoul entity or multidimensional whole of consciousness.

Evolution

Do the strongest really survive
carry on the better progeny
or is it just more favourable
for that part of time
a unique expression influenced of course
by all other surrounding expressions
either survives - because of its uniqueness
or because of its strength - or both
what do all these circumstances create
a few survivors?
stronger in their own unique way
and weaker ones who perish - sacrifices?
so evolution has functioned somehow
as a survival mechanism?

Isn't this nature's way of coping
with the stresses inflicted upon her
she ensures that some
will carry on the life force
I know that nature takes care of all
if we just leave her alone
Mother Earth always regenerates, rejuvenates
and restores balance
so here again is the stop message
stop and listen and appreciate
what we each have
stop and enjoy growth all around and within
stop and celebrate every unique expression
for higher manifestation in our world
and there will be no need
for mere survival

What would be the point if we could not see beyond currently known causes/influences in this world. The theory of evolution is limited in its scope when it does not encompass the idea of conscious emergence. Somehow Earth has survived with lifetimes and dimensional timelines of generation after generation of increasing toxicity and now all has arrived on every plane of existence here with the same condition of heaped-up hereditary patterns or timeline limitations in growth, in all animal and lifeforms on Earth.

We are all together evolving at this time of a great dimensional timeline convergence for a paradigm shift or rebirth for all levels of existence in the Earth planes of existence with the shift to a greater symbiotic or more conscious relationship of exchange between Earth and all in existence here and higher for evermore after for the future of All greater possibilities to come. A step up evolutionary to higher ways for higher conscious beings who are ready, responsible, open and responsive to all in existence, here to bravely embrace a new birthright, with our Earth to higher evolution.

The karmic law of cause and effect is collapsing within 3rd dimensional consciousness of time lines and space realities with a paradigm shift or adjustment we are all incorporating along with our Earth. When we trust our growing clarity of senses or clairsentience - with our twin OverSoul growing connection and greater bond, we gain insights into all our connections here on Earth. And higher, conscious souls begin to do their part to make greater, conscious choices staying open and responsive with their Overbond and for our Earth's unfoldment as she prepares with us, her new higher dimension of connection within the All of creation.

When we trust that the collapse we see in this world is also bringing enlightenment, Love, encouragement for higher choice and opportunities for positive change, then we can begin a new path, a new way and in turn 'step-up' to our evolutionary pathway.

Parenting

Do our children really need us
need us to parent them - I don't know
I think we are trying to make up
for the parenting we never knew - we had
our great parent
Father/Mother Spirit - OverSoul
so we try to parent them
and only end up teaching them - to need us
the way we need a parent
we all need our Over parent - always
only we don't know where to look for it
so as I learn to trust
in my growing OverSoul bond for inspiration
perhaps I can follow my greatest Parent
for and with my daughter
instead of stifling
each of our divine Over connection

Children never lose the connection
but somehow along the way we've forgotten
we were taught to rely on human nature
to survive
instead of our growth in spiritual nature
to flourish

Each OverSoul of pairs' masculine and feminine aspect energies or
the Father/Mother principle within each and all other lifeforms on the
planet have been the parameters of all life in the earthplane. While
each evolving soul aims for ultimate balance of these energies of past
or timelines of experiences for joyful expression; there is a swaying
back and forth between hereditary or lifetime root issues and beliefs
and the conscious, creative urge to merge with the greater expanse of
multidimensional consciousness. And freeing and challenging those
twin separate dimensional experiences to blend together what they
have acquired in much more limiting and restrictive, non-
multidimensional states of many other separate lifetimes. Both halves
of experience from each OverSoul pair are evolving to some greater
expression and union for divine creation of all levels of existence here
in new Earth reality consciousness.

Our OverSoul parent teaches us to become like a child again through our strengthening Overbond of Love. Not to forget that our children need the greatest parent in our example to grow with courage and faith through life's adversities and joy with unbound love. We learn to regain Our underlying ideals and dream again for their highest expressions.

I have always trusted that lightbody Hearts can take on at least some of others' issues because they can always just stay outside the issues and observe - stay OPEN and simply let the energy take care of everything. But I am aware that this is too simplistic in this world presently. And I also know that an open Heart is a very powerful thing indeed - that it can also attract alot of negativity - simple polarity - meaning, a huge magnet for evil too! (I do not mean that like some outside force - just the surfacing of alot of downloaded or stored baggage of patterns in our chakra system (from opposing others and other lifetimes too) - like it all hitting the fan so to speak if one can't offload it/channel it in a naturally healthy way). But this is best if each is allowed the time and space to do so - I am talking about our greater expressions or work but also about when one takes the time to lie down and do some zammin' - full Opening at the Heart meditation.

I've always thought that the lightbody child or youngster (including us) would be able to identify the strange illusions we find ourselves being sucked into at times and that it must be like watching a huge play or something. I've always been aware that this is what is harder for the lightbody parent in the long term - but illusively easier in the short term because the lightbody child would just go along with the illusions we can get stuck in (especially if linked with them on a DNA level or biologically). Unless we deal with issues sooner than later, they would really get stuck too and then we would have to pull for both. (Thankfully though once reaching teenage years, they really start hurling it back more, with puberty full chakra opening initiating - and although it is really challenging, I am grateful. They won't inherently take it on now as much)

Beholden

What is this beauty
on my surface
I have always felt that it is a mask
part of the costume
for a limited role
that I must play in this life
beauty - 'only skin deep'
or does it radiate from within?
so my role has always been skin deep
shallow with no depth of character
I have been expressing only a very small part
just scratched the surface
what lies in the depths
waiting to be explored, believed in - expressed

Sometimes I have thought that I could change
somehow? - when pondering some past time
I could see ease with who I was
but I know now, that it starts from within
and if I truly believe in my beautiful Over beingness
then I can begin to express a new wholeness of beauty
but will I be becoming of all parts - transcend myself
I guess it depends upon what I believe
bout my greater self
beauty - 'in the eye of the beholder'
so I must behold myself or be beholden
hold myself - bound in gratitude
be grateful for all of me - every part
and bind all these true parts or aspects together
blending each our halves'
dimensional aspect lessons consciously
able now to create beautiful expressions of Oneself

Discover these parts
or yin or yan aspects of experience
and allow them to surface in their turn, in time
for All combined aspects blending together
specialities, talents creatively
in Our unique way

The multidimensional aspects of our being yearn to be expressed through a Oneness for completeness. It is in that harmonious experience of Our Entirety that beauty becomes manifest in our life - through us and all around us, as Our part or role within the All-of-creation. Our new multidimensional reality of All dimensionally combined OverSoul strengths here in new Earth reality. And for all a complete higher blending and full incorporation with shared lessons of experience here in Earth's evolving separated astral planes or spiritual layered realm of existence - all growing and evolving together into higher consciousness.

The inner interpretation is of great importance - critical for inspiration and break through mentalities. But if you don't share, you suffer simply because the energy is so incredibly strong - it needs expression. It needs freedom. We can express in so many ways but the creative source needs an outlet so badly everywhere now. It is stifled on so many levels and we think we have enough creative artistic expression in our world and yet we crave it so badly that we are starving ourselves.

There is so much more we need it for all the time and not just for the sake of expression but for inspiring solutions that are needed absolutely everywhere; whether its inspiration for upliftment, for further insight or for actual ideas and concrete applications. (inspiration: the gift of enlightenment and how it feeds even the smallest of details - continuity, emphasis and cohesion of ideas) Creative artistic expression in every facet of life/existence - multidimensional expression for all and every single obstacle for growth/change to higher ways.

This is all about the dynamics of the interplaying of the twin or yin/yan energies of experience from all dimensional timelines of consciousness. Each in twin pairs likely have an equal amount of times in lifetimes in both physical female and male existence while either energy was experienced in either physical form for both. But at this time both in a pair's experiences will need to be integrated for a completeness of lightbody growth for each individual of a pair, although shared or blended at the higher levels all pairs share that completion of balance for Triad rebirth.

Leap with the Dream

I gave up my will to live
long before I hit the bottom
when I hit the bottom I received a vision
something to grasp onto - this was the point
I gave up my will to die
our will is a gift from the Creator
and what it means
is that we have a higher choice
we can choose the way we want to live our lives
choosing the best ways are really Our way
since we are all unique expressions of the Creator
so we can will things to happen in our lives
through and with our Creator if we so choose
or we can deny that higher connection of ourself
deny our will to live - and slowly die

Willing things to happen in one's life
can create miracles
if one accepts the gift - the gift of the will
so accept it, believe it, and live it
I feel quite bold saying my will
can be perfectly aligned
to All of creation's possibility
of wishes, hopes and dreams
could my dreams and hopes ever be that perfect
how badly are they tainted?
could I be setting myself up for a fall - again
here I go again - too afraid to take the leap
leap of faith - that unconditional support
is always there to uplift me each time I fall
learning each time - it's easier to stand up stronger
and how will I ever know if I don't try

Believing in our part of creation is a test of faith, as every decision becomes a conscious choice to grow. We realize this greater free will as the miraculous impact of our part in creations made manifest. The responsibility lies in trust, with Our greater awareness lifting past beliefs/barriers as we uncover original ideals for more clarity of vision for our deepest wishes and dreams.

Talking to Higher Self

Where are you now
where have you been
almost gave up on you
can you believe in me
I don't want any of this
just want to find my way home
no more tricks
get out of my way!
or should I just follow your lead
don't disappear
I can't do it alone
I've tried so hard
only to bury myself slowly
pick me up and carry me
to some place I can - stop
stop my life in its tracks
will you wait for me there?
I don't know how to stop
will you do this for me
and when we meet in this place
maybe we can hold hands
and walk together

An internal battle of inner-balance for growth of our energy system is the difficult way to our higher path - our evolving Higher Self's sparring for ego-transcendence as we seek a straighter, clearer and much higher, Over connected path during the process of upliftment. Trials and errors of all known choices only make the realization of giving-up seem more acceptable, but the real choice to freedom is there all along - clearer, conscious choices within OverSoul partnership for higher living. Our OverSoul enlightens in the midst of our wranglings for a collapse in our known reality as We embrace a better way.

It's so hard for me to imagine that we chose all the difficulties - because we came here? I feel I have put some serious stops in all those old patterns or karmic plans and so lifted 'the veil' of illusionary belief systems.

Memoirs

My whole chest cavity is throbbing or resonating
this feels different from any sensations of energies
that I have felt in the past - in my body or chakras
it is an incredible warming ache - in the centre of my chest
that spreads outward in every direction
I don't know if my heart is changing rhythm
and actually growing in some way
I am sort of scared of this feeling
because I know something very profound is happening
though - I am also excited - I feel the energy with this ache
it started with my meditation last night
I went within completely - only once before, recently

> *I was shown - him again...I took it to mean*
> *he was still confused about me and how I felt about him*

I am swaying between hope
and despair, with no direction
I can't seem to get anything done
without a great deal of effort
I have so much indecision about every little task
where am I going - what am I doing and why
I can't seem to justify anything in my life right now
past or future - I only have feelings these days
nothing concrete but I can't go on feelings alone
I sway back and forth between logic and feelings
weighing one against the other
I have learned in the past few years my feelings are very valid
and I have ignored them for much of my past
but now for the first time - I realize some new truth
that these two must be balanced somehow
with a third - my OverSoul
and I must embrace OverSoul inspiration shining forth
in the midst of my wrangling to unlock my truth

> *why am I so afraid to get to know him*
> *I am back to this question*
> *and of course, I ask myself, why am I so afraid*
> *to get to know and believe in my highest self*

I keep You/my OverSoul at a distance
somehow hoping You will do the work
miraculously melding together, without me even trying
ironically when You came through the first time
I had my guard down
I guess I'll have to let my guard down again

Why do I have such a thick brick guard house around me
why I felt I needed this - I've been trying to protect myself
from anymore hurt or pain - but I've also locked it all inside
I sense this happened when I was a child
I need to know why I have this guard up
I want to break it down so I can love and be loved
please help me to let-go so that my guard will melt
and my greater wholeself can shine forth
I want to know Our twin strengths more personally
be stronger through Our developing
OverChild bond always
I want us to be closer as confidants and friends
with this divine connection I will be honoured - forever

Let this path of discovery be joyful
a celebration as I know it can be
help me to let-go with joy not with pain
I want to discover my Whole self with joy

Listening for the OverHeart's synchronicity in life becomes a lesser task as 'we are joined' through our twin connection by both Over/under Triad bonds and trust in Our multidimensional through our own developing Child inner bond. We find balance within a larger understanding of Ourself. We sway and struggle with the pull of opposing energies of attraction when all the while feeling the pull back to old or familiar ways of habitual reaction with others around us. When we push back or give up trying in each of our lives with the polarizing guard-wall of same aspect limiting issues and patterns of experience within, our twin undersoul-other gets stuck with us instead of trying to gain with exchange in both of our strengths of experience for the same relevant issue - and for all others in our evolution. When we open to Our Lightbody Oneness, we feel its leap with joy.

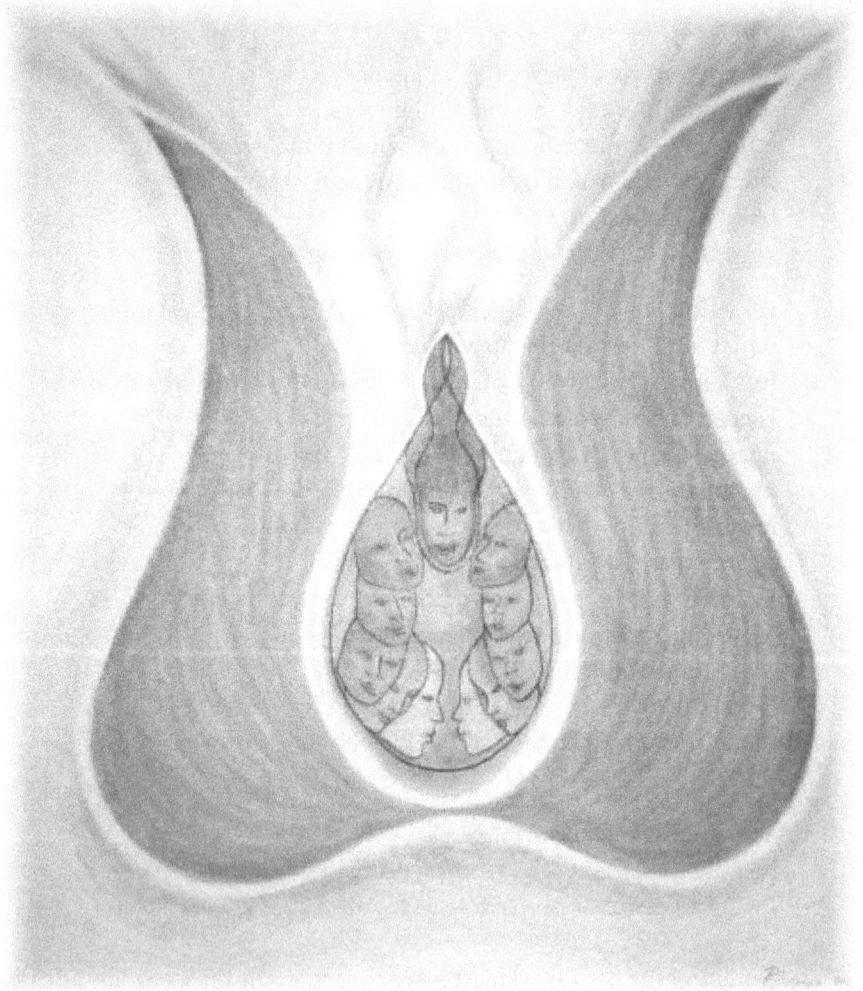

'Twin-Flames' (Oil Pastel and Ink, 15 ³/₄"h x 14"w)

2) We only really recognize synchronicities around us (and hopefully we are getting very adept with interpreting those synchronicities as to what remnant pattern they represent at least) when they are somewhat detached from our consciousness - and that part is somewhat simple enough for multidimensional Lightbodies - in that we are always able to switch perspectives and outlooks (especially when we have the emotional clarity).

Re-cognition of where, who and why they are coming at us - usually a childhood issue being carried for family and friends - the tough ones are family because they are so deeply rooted and friends - from past lives or timelines too - but again we only need to say "Oh, that is a stuck/blocked perspective I didn't even know I had - but now I see where it is coming from and why it was so difficult to be dealt with". Dreamstates, visions, flashbacks, body sensations, aches/pains will also present the synchronistic reoccurance of patterns for a whole enactment to really get the point across dramatically.

Polarizing and Rebalancing

Opposing or Complimentary
Strength of Leanings

Merge with our OverSoul pair bond for higher conscious choices - rebalancing/blending twin aspects of experience;

Fore-shadowing	*To See You Again*
Opening	*Patience*
Let your OverHeart	*Who Am I*
Tuned In	*Twinflames*
Part of We	*Twin Within*
Looking at OneSelf	*My Love*
Remembering	

Path to Higher Manifestation: Third Step
Recognizing past issues/patterns from feedback of synchronistic reoccurances, re-presenting remnants of past collapsing consciousness

Fore-shadowing

What is this fear I sense
what am I so afraid of - is it my past
or many past lifetimes or timelines
some deep dark secret I've buried
or do I just set up this picture
of doom and foreboding
to sabotage my unfoldment

This fear seems to evade me
steer me awry as I get closer to it
do I need to somehow embrace it
or should I just let-go of it
with no recollection of it

I seem to want to understand everything
is this control?
I don't want to do this because I sense
this is what is causing me the greatest pain
I want to surrender with joy in my Heart

Trying to control every step of the evolutionary awakening process is like throwing shadows in your wake. Wanting to 'go after' every shadow to test every part of who we are becoming; yet we are not walking alone when we choose the higher path of unfoldment. While the old habits of waiting to follow synchronistic clues or carrots only stifle and yet we might end up desperately avoiding these same annoying shadows of diversion by running away or going out of our way after tackling every obstacle of limitation with an insecure outlook; instead   we begin with our self-assured trust and with patience in the process of growth for intuitive guidance of clarity.

Fears need not stifle if we no longer acknowledge or act upon them as such and re-cognize patterns of limitation by acting only on the relevant issue that is limiting our progression at any one time. Our works are honed out of these experiences and carry us forward through each passing phase as we incorporate newly combined layers of consciousness. Surrendering from such a lonely stance, we begin courageously trusting in the larger, shared dance that brings Our Entirety into play.

Opening

I have always sensed
that we are kindred spirits
I have felt a very strong
and special connection to you
I hope you can forgive me
for not finding the courage
to get to know you as a true friend
would know the love that you need
for I know in my Heart
that you are a very special person
I hope you feel this
for if you don't - you are missing out
on the greatest Love
this life has to share
Love of Oneself

Let your OverHeart
blaze out your path before you
and may you shine with this Love
every step of the way

When our Heart-flame recalls Our twin, inner struggles for balance
and freedom, we have the opportunity to awaken more fully to the
greater exchange taking place. When issues are identified and old fears
of our own restricting patterns lift with our choice to move forward, a
higher exchange of aspect energy of experience or filtering of newly
combined strength of leaning blends for us.

We then open to our greater bond with the knowledge of past
limiting habits and with OverHeart perspective follow a higher path
with new strengths incorporating within us and determination to
release ourselves from protective or competitive stances. With our
greater conscious choices for growth comes enlightenment, as we
open-to and expand with Our greater Love - that shines clearer with
each step in our awakening.

Tuned In

I am getting better at listening
but I am not always sure I want to hear
I had trouble with listening
from early on I heard
"she's very quiet,
does not volunteer her thoughts and feelings"
I guess I was in my world of day dreams
and remember coming back
I don't know how far I drifted
'in my own little world'
but I must have needed it
for my so-called real world

I've listened to others telling me
'pay attention', I must have a hearing problem
well they were absolutely right
what I was hearing - didn't get through
learning that listening to others well
meant tuning in what they're not
the language of symbols
underlying truths of spoken word

I am tired of listening
to people who justify their living-lies
somehow - mostly to themselves
I listen to what others don't want to listen to
but they're the ones who need their truth...

If others are not asking for help consciously
then karmic obligatory felt giving
or receiving overrides
and does not incorporate greater growth and change
it is one's own purity of intension
or best wishes
and the follow through of a letting go of expectation
for a process of trust
brings the Universe's best manifest responses
for all our requirements of experience
for true growth

We become more fine-tuned with our growth in consciousness as we embrace Our greater awareness or clearer-sensing. Our sensitivities gradually and gracefully develop as we acknowledge our links or ties with others - acting on our knowings by sharing with reverence to others but become more responsible for all through our example of growth.

We trust that any exchange of information for us can come for consequently all and from all around this Earth. How we choose to impart the intuitive knowings through Our OverHeart connection builds as Our special bond grows - with our Over partnership through conscious incorporation of all relevant experiences and greater conscious choices.

Our growing bond of trust in the greater evolutionary process moves us to higher dimensions of consciousness. This bond can build with personal interpretations of language of symbols that represent past or any timeline concepts from the larger karmic pool of global groups of consciousness. They present themselves through dimensional synchronistic reoccurrences or events that represent/mirror past or any timeline remnant shadows/reflections of patterns and beliefs - direct feedback from all breaks consciously in dimensional timeline but personal groups' set of karmic prechoices; always linked to a timeline as we are forever in the now/present - bridging for the highest visions of the future.

Never assume the masses are so unaware or unawake. Everyone is waking now, moving higher and everyone needs the language of personalized symbolism for their interpretation of the truth - their own experiences of such, being of prime importance.

We are disrespectful to ourselves and others when we do not trust in a greater communication. When we do not work out our own anger at the world but mostly we are not respecting others enough to know that their experience and understanding is there contribution and is of utmost importance for an overall exchange in the mass consciousness - working together consciously with issues that are truly shared for higher manifest solutions for many in our lives.

Part of We

When You call me I know its You
but I'm not sure of my role
an instrument, a partner
I feel in the way, most times
nudge, push - call and I follow
and how beautiful the outcomes
but how do 'we' contribute?
is this new me - mostly You
why did I forget You
this out of some false sense of duty or guilt
was this the plan?
or was it so that large scale growth was possible
but if OverSouls re-membered altogether
in waves of growth for all
of time and space reality here
We wouldn't want to get in the way!

Remembering...
we're One - when a child
only to start over and over with each life
remember, forget, remember...
surely You did not want this
so now we go - into our rightful place
this new place - is it truly all of Ours
OverSouls of pairs all together for us here?
for Our new Earth reality
are we here because we couldn't get there
without All
what is Our part within creation

Each developing Overself or twin underSoul has a myriad of both masculine and feminine past or timeline personality of self traits or specialist identities and exchanges information dimensionally through their OverSouls for any needed combined complimentary input; never presenting more to us than needed for present challenge or are conducive for growth. Reidentifying and reintegrating any aspect/identity of either energy triggers a rebalancing or exchange of the twin-energies within. Where one gravitates normally towards one side of expression in energy of experience or belief system on any relevant issue more easily and readily, the less personally dominant of opposing or complimentary aspect-energy of either masculine or feminine perspective from our OverSouls (and pooled from OverSouls linked to teams of karmic groups with similar dynamic issues and patterns) gradually and increasingly starts to take on new expression in one's life to balance this past old strength of leaning or tendency.

While one may feel a sort of reidentification with a more suppressed side or dimensional aspect of themselves or with our twin-other view that is needing greater understanding within us through outward expression, we find the opportunity for healing/growth with this new perspective for any current limitation presently challenging us. We learn to trust in an incorporation for opportunity of previously learned experience with this view for our growth and greater exchange of a new combined lesson of experience as we adapt within to the challenge. And we fully embrace our new combined strength or overall growth in each energy with either more whole masculine or more whole feminine incorporation at any given period, as this whole new process of re-membering uplifts.

We are all growing so profoundly and yet we can't seem to trust that we are All doing this together. Everyone just wants to blame. They look around and seeing the extremes think many are either out-of-it or crazy. We are ignoring others because of cynicism and blame; not taking any responsibility for change or trying so hard to change that we close ourselves in our own determination and become disconnected for awhile. Either way it makes it hard to open-up and trust others, share and be willing to learn that dance of interpretation (fine-tuning) with others.

Do any of us want to be judged as someone strange. Maybe so, if we honestly believe it is the only way we can express ourselves openly and truthfully. I believed that my interpretations of my new realities/truths were not really my own - that somehow they were there and only coming through to help others. Actually I needed to internalize them first, incorporate them, make them my own and trust that was the purpose - all facets for growth coming together as I share with others - feedback for myself and for others' somehow too.

Looking at Oneself

It's like I'm a mirror
always reflecting back to people
some new part they see in themselves
only when they truly look into this mirror
they rarely see the real me
they see someone else - just castings off
I'm always someone else - to everyone
I am never - just me
how could I ever expose
my true identity
no one would ever understand
no one ever has
and whenever I feel - finally
someone is beginning to understand
I change again
and throw them off completely
why can't I find - someone
just one
who could change when I change
synchronicity - is this possible
with another human being?
I know You will always understand me
but that's different
You are my voice and my ears
this kind of understanding
surpasses any form of communication
between individuals
telepathic or otherwise

Dialoguing with Oneself brings peace and greater trust as One changes so profoundly through awakening. Others may perceive little of this happening/change as exterior reflections or synchronistic reoccurances contradict and higher manifestation lapses in time. But the rebalancing and blending of the twin-energies of experience within is the priority for new recognition of Oneself and the celebration we share most specially, through our Lightbody Triad development.

Remembering

I am mourning a loss
something lost years ago
I am trying to reclaim it
my youth, my vulnerability, my spontaneity
my openness to life
I closed off more than my Heart back then
I rejected everything real in my life
and now that reality is being reawakened
I am re-experiencing joys under those memories
a joyous way that was blocked-out under trauma

I am youthful again
with all the challenges of being youthful
the playfulness with abrupt shocks
the bouncing back
the experimenting - carefully at first
and then more haphazardly
only to trip-up again but stand up
each time stronger
but all the while with a sense of humour
because I cannot judge myself
I am like a new student to life
maturity is only felt in the moment
when you can laugh at yourself
and see yourself - truly renewed in strength
in our greater continuum
of all shining moments

Our past holds timely keys through awakening, but not to recall like cycles forgotten. Only in the moment with Our higher choices, do we rise to the challenge of stumbling 'blocks', for the child of our youth - unlocking/redeeming layers at origin of fear, where they link firmly rooted. And we are released to face current challenges with new clarity of purpose through layers of blockage, for growth - a collapse/clearing within karmic record occurring as memory is forever reshaped and we reignite with the lost glories of ideals from childhood - Our newly found truths! Forever in the now, do we most profoundly stay clear through Our continuum as we move higher with all dimensional timeline memories and visions of the future.

To See You Again

What is that

shining in your eyes

love or just tears

like mine

dripping like salt

into wounds

when will I see

past this welling of pain

obscuring my visions

Our deepest wounds/blockages unleash the most profound healings in our Heart-flame's re-membering/blending. But while pain is endured, the emotional blockage only blinds. Opening to our OverHeart connection completely and surrendering, regenerates Our Over Love, as it surges its way out - redeemed; engulfing the emotional pain we've held onto like guilt. And where past wounds scarred, now only an opening cleared for deeper connection.

A continual connection that has always served to wake us up and move us higher for our ever renewed pathway. The connection can never hold one of an underSoul pair back. If the energy stagnates both break it up together at the higher levels. An energy clash only pushes each on or pulls each forward. Each automatically helps the other with their own relevant half view to any limiting issue in their respective world when trusting that the energy serves both equally. And we can develop a comfort with the connection 'through the dimensions' while having a harder time understanding it in the here and now. We are trusting in the connection even if we are not aware of it the way the other may interpret it in this linear dimension of time.

We all grope and desperately cling at times for help. We don't want to do this to others. We want to stand up and shine - be strong and steady in our move forward in life and with all issues challenging us. And we realize we never move forward alone. We may have always seen this and known this but we slowly begin to truly believe this as a basic Universal truth! If we do our best though, we shine out for others in a helping way that is beyond anything understandable or fathomable in a newly emerging multidimensional reality.

We begin to understand that it involves many we are linked to especially close lightbody friends. If any are struggling with a particular issue then we are all contributing in a certain way of our own and to how well that flow from Universal change washes through us all. We gradually see more and more how we work through any ultimately global issues together somehow.

The only real help Lightbodies have offered for each other pair in close company so far is that they have pooled their energies and accelerated the issues for All concerned. But of course it can be excruciating especially when we mainly were focusing on help with our immediate physical waking state daily life. But when we focus on maintaining our Complete Parent OverSoul within oneself through our connection we do so for All concerned on all levels! -- to lean on our Triad connection foremost and centre - the 'bond of love' each of a pair conceived a few lifetimes ago.

Patience

I see this love
a true commitment of the OverSoul pairs
only in symbols and barely noticeable

This love is too deep
to be seen by others
it surfaces at times with the serpent rising
wave upon wave
until swept out of time and place
to be with you
entwined with Oneness - such glory
we share Oneness in the same
Overlove bond
but we remain separate
between here and Our higher reality
until more conducive time and place

Patience is not bound by time
true patience I feel
in the moment
we are connected
through all of time
through OverSouls' bond

When Love for the Oneness-of-being is truly embraced through our higher connection, it becomes a catalyst for change, bringing the polarizing of primal energies - drawing on each significant other's strengths of leaning. And a critical shift for balance achieved during the momentum of the Kundalini force - for further complimentary blendings of masculine and feminine aspect energies.

A developing shared Oneness gradually begins shaping Our new reality consciousness as we carry on and move with a chosen pathway while bridging for All between the two realities of higher truth and knowledge and this changing old world consciousness in our physical reality. And higher development through our OverSouls' loving patience with each in a pair of individual unfoldments and devotion to the ever increasing Triad-bonds of Love we are building for each other - for this time of Lightbody evolution.

We might tend to try to figure out where our twin--other is at, at times. One cannot assume or expect anything (but we do!? unfortunately) because it might feel like it should be like starting to meet someone for the first time - good especially because we don't need to pick up the past and rehash it. Our past lessons of experiences are exchanged only - not rehashed - carried for each other with compassion of experience - lessons of incorporation.

Probably will not know what is exchanged in those times of having talked or linking with them thoughtfully - but it helps to collapse - let go of our rigid mentalities with past understanding and experiences of relationship. It is our assumptions that are our own story - what we understand really. We have difficulty staying in our truth so we bounce off each other. We can shrink from our truth and in desperation seek balance through reaching out to our tf logically or illogically. But while we don't want to hide anything from them - for them to know our challenges and doubts, our strengths are always there. Herein lies our greatest truth - when we let our openness carry us over to something more genuine and honestly simple.

Don't assume because we have completely opposite experiences and now all lessons to exchange for this life of lightbody triad - so we don't really know their outlook and they don't really get ours until the exchange of each other's limiting issues starts to take place. (which quite often occurs with much clarity when we are put in each other's shoes in the dreamstate)

Staying aware of yin or yan expression at any given time is really significant when we find ourselves at a dead end course. If you think of it as a slight ripple in any dimensional timeline perspective then you can use this to bring about a 'switch' or a way of bringing back balance to something that has 'stale-mated' because it needs input from 'the other' leaning. We have amongst many dimensional timelines both the yin and yan of our own layers of experience but it is still only our half views or usual tendencies to solve problems - but with our triad bond we can link at a whim to any 'seeable' or perceived hint coming from the dimensional myriad of clues (presenting breakthroughs consciously) by staying clear and alert to timely possibilities.

Who am I

I'm just a fledgling
my soul trying to unleash
I do not have the strength
to wrestle with You
all I can do is fall down
and rest in Your glow
You overcome me now
Your strength is great
You are my strength
I succumb to Your will
and You take care of me
I'm not sure where I am going
what You have in store for me
but I always have Your comfort now
before I even realize
how badly I need it
this love washes over me
cleanses, renews, uplifts, carries me
onward and upward
I have small deaths every day
I get tossed around
only to find
I can regain my balance much better now
but still, where do I choose
it seems 'I' have stopped choosing
I'm just changing - always

The awakening of the Kundalini force brings profound and gentle ripplings of calming and comfort as it fulfils its evolutionary mission of multidimensional blendings of Triad Lightbody. A whole new remembering process begins within each of pairs altogether for higher living and expression. Our individual openings to surrender and acceptance of profound growth is the gift that We give to each other as we find acceptance and embrace the greater exchange - as ongoing living practise and openings through Our OverLove/Child bond of connection to each other, clear channels to brighter tomorrows.

We make assumptions. It made it easier in our mind initially - like we already knew our twin from a past life and we could somehow meet again and get to know one another again; easier too because it felt safer. And then we could ignore how much we are truly drawn to and yet frightened of them - of what we have felt so strongly - that it overwhelmed us all the time - what we come to understand as the OverLove bond.

Part of the fear was the idea - that they are so/too familiar! It is always an adventure meeting new people - this is the key, with no preconceptions their is freedom. But the One eventually does becomes a stranger essentially because as we adapt they no longer feel familiar outside of self, instead with growth they begin to feel inseparable in terms of the issues. Because we each change so profoundly as we incorporate our opposite for combined strength. We become more similar - this is the comfort we feel about ourself as we become more confident and begin to become like what we need to attract; One true for us.

But we are twins - still separate for the most part, supporting each other through opposing/opposite energies - neither exclusive to each. 'When two become One Triad' is a very simple statement. I think that Triad third or combined OverChild consciousness conceived or bonded lifetimes ago for twin-Lightbodies but that true 'coming-together' consciously or birth is not Complete for any of us. I don't know what that will mean exactly for us but think we'll finally be able to live in higher community in Earth plane reality. And I don't think that will come 'completely' for any of us very soon - at least not the way we relate presently in this world - at least, I sure hope not.

Any concept of Triad that I have even tried to perceive/ imagine still seems obscure? Maybe that is something too great that we are still building, creating, evolving as we continue to grow in consciousness. And as we recognize the casts/roles - but mostly, recognition of the Love that is never camouflaged by the roles; we are merging 12 greater roles of each of our separate OverSouls that are becoming 12 Combined greater purposes - balanced to form ONE between each of a pair/ two, Triads in Completion.

Twinflames

When was I like you
you felt so familiar from the start
you could never hide from me
the way I saw you try
this so familiar to me
I thought only I was capable
of such manoeuvring

But there you were
crossing lines into territory
no other had ever ventured
and so gracefully
directly into my Heart
more courageous than myself - at first
you seemed more comfortable there with me
than I did in my own skin around you?

You opened to this Heart connection
with seemingly little effort
a look - a smile
a tone in your voice - resonated within me
even your movements, your mannerisms
could not hide the obvious reflections I saw
reflections of some other time
and from some distant times and places

You and I seem so much the same
on the inside
and yet the world reacts to us so differently?
was I ever like you and you like me?
were we split from Oneness
when did a rejoining begin
and when will it end for twins
when Triad pairs join here

When the path of two meet in the Heart, twin-connection, an immediate exchange of energy unfolds. Recognition of the real bond of Love for the 'One' is felt inside as exterior personas may fool and hide true aspects. Ironically the synchronistic familiarities or patterns that initially draw attention to one another are also the past separately experienced limiting issues that camouflage your 'realness' from one another. But this 'real' magnetism is the pull of that bond of Love and the simultaneous push of polarizing resistance of relative issues surrounding each in their known worlds. Both play out at the higher exchange of the bond, as each rises above or clears through all limiting issues in their respective lives - for twin OverSoul evolution and Triad joining - and for all others in their lives as multidimensional aspects reveal themselves gradually, in faith and trust.

We learn to let go of karmic personality trends carried over from previous or other parallel or even future time experience. They must all wash out until recognition is only our comfort with lightbody oneness - it is a clean slate. We only need to look at our understanding of our connection at times to move higher.

We will attract illusionary twin relationships for growth. One must recognize their own issues in these relationships and not confuse them with their true match's life. As long as we keep those relationships in perspective, aware that we have attracted them for growth - as it always applies to the priority of relevant issues that need playing out for one's own recognition of a limiting half view in relationship - there can be greater growth.

We can't stand up now
we are still too complacent about a past
or other parallel or all timeline consciousness
that clings limiting our freedom
where is the recognition now?
limiting patterns rooted firmly
but jarred loose by recognition

Twin Within

Who do they see in you and I
why do they see our differences
and not our similarities
yes our differences are so blatant
but we share Oneness in the same Overbond
with different territories
in the outer world
we seem to be from two different worlds
of experience, background and understanding
but these appearances
are in our Earth everywhere
worlds colliding - starting anew

Maybe it could be easier for you and I
if we could just remember
we are from the same world
same mind and spirit
I want to remember you
and I hope you will remember me
the parts I have forgotten
about myself and you

While our OverSoul connection is our link with All, we share this special connection through our OverSoul to 'twin-other' OverSoul. And with opposite aspects or backgrounds of experience in lifetimes we having already begun or been in the bond-of-Love in a few other lifetimes of togetherness. A continuous connection since remeeting in this life serves as a catalyst for change with a constant exchange or support through blending of complimentary yin/yan aspect energies for relevant information from a great many past or other time half view separate experiences; that are now much needed to initiate changes within us that allow us to adapt with this transition of collapse in stagnation of time lines of consciousness within the evolutionary paradigm shift of this known world. Able to move on to higher ways as illusions or stifling belief systems fade as we become clearer/lighter as we shed or cast-off patterns and issues of lifetimes and our OverSoul Triad merging is more complete.

My Love

You cut to me open deeper

deeper than I have ever opened to myself

deeper than anyone ever has

because no other erupted from Source within

no other ever connected

with those depth of strengths of my being

depths untouched and forgotten by myself

until you

Our connection through our bond with the 'One' so significant-underSoul-other triggers openings of the deepest kind. Wounds carrying the patterns of heritage from timelines of consciousness and blocking information of incarnations of experiences together that are holding the keys to awakening for all One's connections are pulled and redeemed, as our greater Love continues to emerge. Emotional concepts of love rise to higher levels as they wash through for cleansing with our greater Overbond of Love.

> **feelings** - *often felt with entanglement of association between extremes of built-up emotion - from cut-off suppressed feeling to burst of release of over-reaction.*
> **knowing** - *just a certainty of something anywhere from vague to more certain awareness.*
> **intuitive knowing** - *emotional clarity of knowing or inspirational awareness, linking through Heart with mind.*

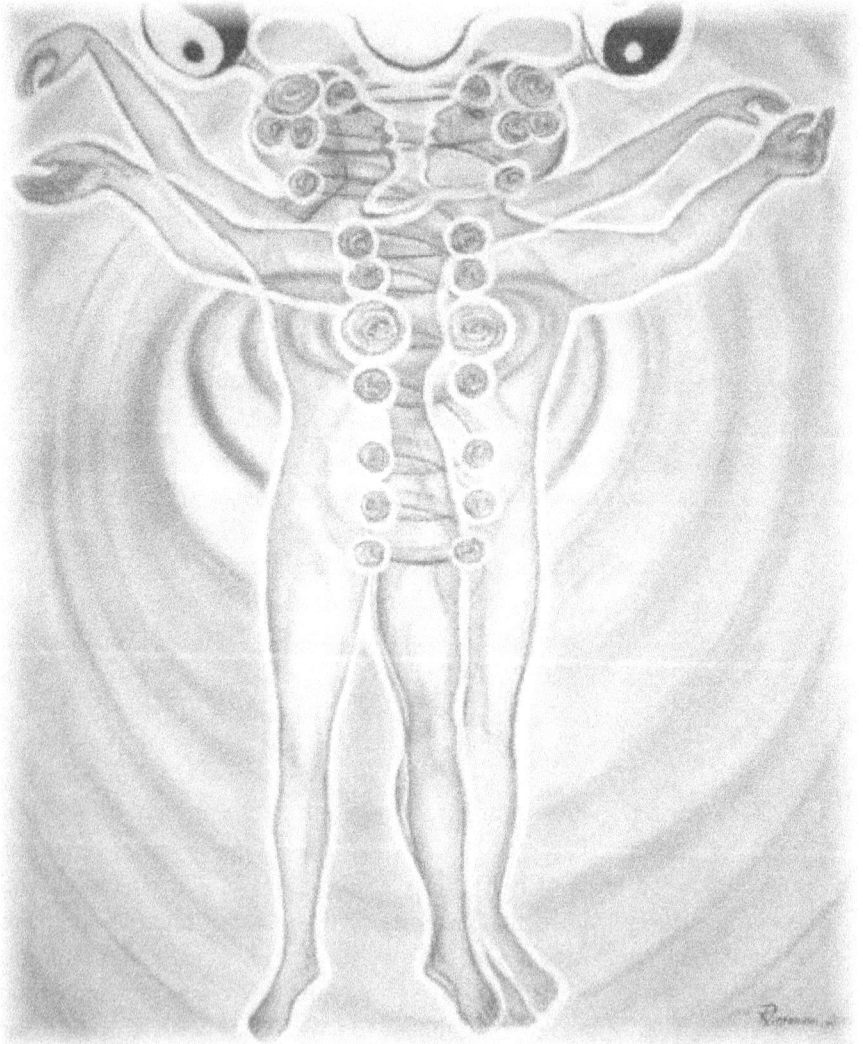

'Lightbody'   (Soft Pastel and Charcoal, 17"h x 14"w)

3) The other part is not even the recognition of the issues though. Manifesting is after we recognize the issue bringing us already halfway there - but the Key then is that we can truly start, by essentially walking away from old taunts/carrots OR annoying demands that we really don't want either but keep badgering us.

This part is very critical because it exercises our conscious Choice for Change! We can waver a little only to see the synchronicities start to flare up again - but it is getting critical now because everything is accelerating so fast and is so chaotic around us at times. So we have less room for doubt all the time. (walking away is still necessary even in the next phase sometimes, if you don't take a real stand initially.) But it gets clearer to us all the time as we begin to cast off layers or detach consciously while incorporating new strengths.

Forging

Collapse within the Emotional Realm

Forge our greater bond standing with higher choices;
see ego-walls collapse for new beginnings for OverSoul pairs

My Child's Dream	*Encouragement*
Child	*I Love You*
Children know	*My Light-Body*
Sisters	*Light Workers*
This Joining	*This is The Point*
A New Beginning	*Assumptions*
Vulnerability	*I know now*

Path to Higher Manifestation: Fourth Step
Exercising conscious choice for change with emotional/mental clarity,
making a stand for your choice to move higher

My Child's Dream

"You're throwing sand in my eyes"
Who's throwing sand in your eyes?
"You are"
You're dreaming
"It's not a dream. Its real. You're really doing it"
Dreams are real. I'll stop. I won't do it again.
"You can throw it when I go inside...
when I'm there..."
That's what I did
I went inside myself
when they threw sand in my seeings
I just went inside
I knew it was o.k. for them to throw sand
I could just stay inside
but I don't want my wounded child to stay inside!
and I don't want to discount what I see
for myself or anyone

When will I come out completely?
when will this hiding stop
who do I think I'm hiding
or running away from
can I not recognize myself at all - any part?
this is more of me - who We are becoming now
take it or leave it
I don't have to leave it anymore

I need more time to stand up, full front, exposed in my truth
because I know - they are going to throw
more than sand - this time
and maybe they would not have
if I hadn't let them all these years

This is more than just me
this is everything - this is the future
this is Our choice - of clear-seeing - clairvoyance
mine and others - and All
can see from that same place deep within
we find Our Shangri-La when we reach within

and when we find it, we know
we are reaching the beginning
of a whole new way of living on this Earth
we find our greater connection there
or the beginnings of what We can truly be
whole, complete, truly joyful for the first time
with no big surprises to convince us
just learning, relaxing and being Oneself effortlessly

The only struggle is letting go of the old Self
the one we thought we were so well
the one with the massive ego around our wounded child
but letting go of the ego's protective stance on life
and allowing it to get down to a more rightful perspective
is no easy journey
I just keep saying "we grow or suffer" - little choice here
but the Soul has little choice - with ego-walls
so we go through ego-bashings
until the OverSoul finally shine's through
for the real you - humbled you

When you get to that point you're better able at listening
truly with inner hearing, seeing or knowing
then you begin to really feel your OverSoul bond
you get excited at the outpouring of love
for you - a love that envelopes you
until you know it's just the more Whole you - more real you

The Soul reaches the point where scars of under-layering wounds clear enough for the surfacing of our inner-child. Wounds unprocessed at times of layered trauma, buried for our protection, have opened with awakening. A breaking down of ego stirs an upheaval of emotion that washes to the surface to respond for healing. The inner-child seeking fuller expression in the outer world feels the weight of emotional blockages of heritage from generations and all incarnations of timelines and struggles to courageously detach from a once safe perspective to one much safer/higher in vibration. The great flood threatens to overcome; only with choices for the path of Our evolving Heart does One ascend, as such turbulence clears from passages in time, along with the Kundalini force, for the initiate child's emergence.

Child

Children are shining examples
of what should be
unhindered
open to life
ready to show us the way
a completely joyful way
into the future
as simple as their playful ways
and their fondest dreams
Oh to be like a child
and believe again
and feel again - the full outrage
from an assault on that belief system

They look to us to say
it can change
it can be better
we can start again

Children know
about beginnings
they begin everything they do!

The open, powerful OverChild of our Earth beams an array of hope for a new place within all Hearts. Beyond the wounds in time, lies the source of strength in Our developing OverChild bond; our true caregiving through divine wisdom. Beginning again in us; we move into higher consciousness with Our evolving, loving example of growth through joyful interplay of the blendings of divine energies of experiences - through clear/open emotional expression - open and powerful enough to express inner truth and beauty for a new world of higher evolution.

I have learned something about what it means to be strong - from others. I have been there for lightbodies I guess and I know they have been there for me. But it seems like we (lightbodies) haven't really known that ultimate test? I mean, we know about being vulnerable to carry on in our own light. But for others who are awakening all around us now to some greater degree, they are really tested now too. I can see it in their eyes and overall tone of expression. They recognize and feel our gaping vulnerability and it makes them really uncomfortable - but they know with their Hearts that it is a great test for them somehow too? - to make every effort to pay attention in the moment. So they have taught me this really - and it's so scary at times and powerful too because I have learned I have to put my truth into their hands in the moment, especially and simply because I have chosen something important and new. They recognize that and it frustrates them and they appreciate it too at some level.

Ironically, I've always wanted to be the one who is there for others (most of my past) but it seems it hasn't been my call right from the beginning of my accelerated awakening. I always have tried to do more for others but it has been just enough for me to focus and learn to trust and LET others do for All - for all Our parts together somehow? And this continues to test me still?

The key is childlike belief and faith and wonder and excitement. Yes, there is also stubbornness too at times because of all our childlike protective scars and therefore rigid stances in life that need to collapse. And that can be scary at times. But our Lightbody development really takes care of all that as We build that 'bond of trust'!

That 'bond of trust' is a big part of the Combined OverSoul or developing OverChild consciousness. How can it be that the traumatized/ inner child can be part of this too? - because as we clear out all the issues in our lives 'together', rooted in childhood, we strengthen each of our inner child bond to ultimately complete our Over Triad bond in this lifetime. (growing trust between pairs = combined OverSoul) The healing inner child for each of a pair is in incubation and has been since our true-match bond was first conceived. We have been incubating/ building and growing with our OverLove bond for a long time - through all the layers of consciousness.

Sisters

There was nothing I could give you
I did not know how to give
what I could not give myself
I was not strong enough for me
to be of any help to you
I needed to shine myself out
fully enough to really feel
my own reflections
and to know it was really me - wholly
multidimensionally
that I was feeling
maybe now my more wholeSelf can be teacher
now with my Overbond example
this love of a new OverSoul Child
not yet completely born here within

When we discover that the one last refuge lies within the sanctity of our OverHeart connection, we begin the process of wounded/inner-child growth and nurture through our divine Source. Leaning on Our OverSouls' bond through The All-of-creation, we learn a new walk as our Overbond connection gradually begins to forge/cement for our new multidimensional incorporations with combined, blended strengths gradually beginning to reroot in our consciousness. We begin to grow/expand with further yin/yan chakra activations, initiations of our Lightbody development - and we teach messages of hope when we shine out our truth, in example.

How do I know that we are not at the point of this great Birth between each pair of twins (that any pairs are near this yet) - simply because of the traumatized or inner child we carry over lifetimes or through timelines. Each of our incubating/ growing Combined OverChild consciousness is still carrying for and with each in a pair of us. ('The Child of Light' - this Child and the inner child in each are not really separate) It cannot come to completion until we are truly 'together' consciously, when the issues have been cleared-out totally ('holding hands walking into the light') It is yet to be seen how this will interpret/unfold.

This Joining

This time is the last time
or is just the beginning
of yet another kind of journey
for you and I
will you walk a new path with me
will you brave a new reality
treading gracefully over new ground
new dimensions unfold
look up and see where relatively few others have gone
and now we follow and lead by example
here and in higher reality
each individually with our OverSelf development
a partnership within
and with Our OverChild Oneness
a partnership with one another
hand in hand, bonding with Our Overlove
altogether with pairs
into a new world consciousness

Primal, twin-energies stabilize through the momentum of the Kundalini Force, continuing to nourish and comfort through this process of unfoldment. Each brave step brings new awareness as we clear the way for each of Our new, OverChild perspectives. Each newly developing Combined OverSoul or OverChild incubates while both developing, corresponding or 'underSouls' evolve beyond their twin-paths and altogether in purpose they merge composite energies of their multidimensional aspects towards a new reality of Triad pairs of Lightbody.

Every human on the planet now and those that have ever existed in this reality does and has had a traumatized Child. (or what is commonly referred to as the Inner Child. It is simply the way it has been here - never really been a safe or conducive place for children throughout history) We only need recognition of the issues associated with original traumas (having been layered over many lifetimes or through timelines) to release enough energy for us to move ever higher consciously, enough for washout of each layer. But how many layers left?

A New Beginning

What Child is this?
the new hope for this earth
the new life breath
from the universe
welcome brave Light-being
You have answered our call upon You
and we've felt Your gentle persuasion
urging us - from the beginning
Our courageous Hearts
have brought us together
to blaze out new paths for this generation
guide us gently little One
teach us a new way
with Your shining example
we each begin together with You

Our initiation into a new multidimensional reality brings in the new order with the merging of the OverChild of We-consciousness. Each higher Overself is now strong enough and now able to fully house the incorporation of combined multidimensional aspects of twin OverSoul pairs. A new emerging OverSoul consciousness is now more complete with Triad developing OverChild bonds. This new WholeSelf, directed advantage breathes new life into the best of old realities.

Lightbodies are not ready to exchange in harmony in their day to day waking reality until their 'joining' with their twin-partner or Triad completion - not really capable to appreciate and simply enjoy each other's company because of the priorities with all the chaos in this world. I believe, and have always thought that these Joinings are imminent. I still feel that but the unforeseen layers just keep surfacing! So I do not know how long or how many on the planet will do this now or with each wave to come either. Maybe the special number of 144,000 is a clue to how many in waves of lightbodies to move on higher (even prophecies are evolving! - so probably many more)

Vulnerability

Where is this warrior woman
I'm not sure I can defend myself
without her
am I strong enough to go on
without her?
You say I do not have to be tough
to be strong
who will shield me from my own rage
must I always go to war with You
I cannot hide from You
You find me out
and make me look deeper still
until I cannot hold down
all this unspent emotion
from my past or other timelines

Don't let them push me around
how do they see my uncertainty
my confusion
my awkwardness, my vulnerability
like vultures they swoop-in
this Heart needs a protector
where are You
I know You will make this and more
so much easier for me
if I just let You
well then, let them all have it
whatever they are crying for
and let me be free at last
free to be open and vulnerable

Ego-transcendence carries 'warrior' to 'light', as the collapse in timelines of consciousness allows surrender and frees our evolving Heart to gape to its most open and connected state. From this vantage, emotional entanglements/blockages rise with Our higher choices; this battle for balance rises with the expansion of our emerging Overself.

Encouragement

Brave is... allowing yourself to feel scared
when one is brave or courageous
they have allowed their fear
to move up and through them
until it is all around them
so that they can finally recognize
that it is their very own shadows
dancing around them
mocking them, teasing them
coercing them into allowing their emotions
to finally react to this stimuli - this fear
to move them forward - into action
and release their tears, their anger
their bitterness, their resentment
for higher clearing or channel for higher works
so that fear can be consumed
in the utter outrage
of a now blazing Heart connection

The Over Self is able to transform our fears
into enlightenment
so that we can receive the inspiration
the understanding - the tool we need
to propel us through any problem or challenge
with encouragement
and with Overself assurance
fear then no longer paralyses
but is transformed into responsible action
directed through our OverHeart
a Heart that can now feel again
the sheer excitement
of rekindled hopes and dreams

Everyone has signed up for the karmic matrix of predetermined rules of engagement just to come here. The links that bind us to pretold stories that yet need to be played out in turns, over and over again if necessary for some to gain because others sacrifice growth in lifetimes.

Each group consciousness carries karmic patterns that each share a specific signature that is their half view to overall patterns or beliefs that need the full shared Over perspective to bridge or free themselves from endless entrapment of limiting behavioural re-enactments.

Moving beyond karmic reality means moving into Lightbody consciousness. Karma is the ruling factor to rewrite or clear in our lives and where one has carried karmic issues and patterns in all their lives, they lift with lightbody awakening to fuller awareness. Our part is simple enough to pass the torch as we bridge realities for all we are carrying for and linking-to dimensionally, still clouded by past or dimensional timeline karmic world consciousness.

Each Lightbody has an evermore set of patterns and beliefs that lift when they keep their focus on their own limiting view in all cases, to avoid the karmic blame game that is ever threatening. They carry a whole set of responsibilities with their unique part along with other lightbodies doing their part as we all are going through each phase of awakening to higher consciousness. We cannot help each other in tangible ways as each has their own set or pieces of a puzzle that can only be 'filled in' through our own OverSoul bond through growth.

We learn to trust in this growth in bond to know when and what is helpful to share and when it is not and more of a hindrance for all involved. If our challenging other half of any relevant complimentary group lessons are not incorporated consciously then we miss the other half of perspectives for completion of any issue to unlock or lift.

Every issue carries a full dimensional range or layers of perspectives with input that can come through from within or from anyone or synchronistically, from either a yin or yan leaning. Lightbodies process on many dimensional levels of consciousness at once and weave information together at the higher dimensions - in moments in time when needed for new experience of growth with any given issue or belief.

The emotional blockages/build-up of our heritage from generations of our past and timeline incarnations has a purpose now to surface - the full range of emotions help cleanse/clear with the surfacing of shadows or patterns as we respond to challenges around us for change and growth. Our Lightbody development holds keys to enlightenment, for responsible and right-time and place actions to unfold in the moment of need. Under volition/guidance, each act of courage cleanses through the fire, making the way home brighter for All.

I Love You

and I wonder

if I love You

because you poured your Love

out for me

and as words left me

You felt them

and knew it must be true

because they came back to You

they were Our interplay of words

all along

this Overbond of Love

is finally coming back together for us

When Love is One in the same, who is the giver and who the receiver? Returning home to a Oneness is embracing a Love that always was but is re-blended for all time. A merging of composite energies into the developing Oneness of the greater Love of a forged OverHeart. Our developing Triad bond between OverSouls of a pair - a bond of Oneness at the higher levels through Lightbody development before the final tri-bond completion here in new multidimensional physical reality.

My Light-Body

I feel it so strongly
this big shift or change - within me
there is something very profound
happening to me
and my understanding is very personal...

It is - my creative essences
shining through!
not coming from anywhere outside of me
not coming from anything foreign to me
just me - the real me
and I think it's my OverSoul - just ecstatic
and finally - evolutionary speaking
it's time!
it's time for us all to shine together
and it wants to be here
it wants to call this place - Earth - home
and it wants to do that in the human form
it wants to do that with a flesh Lightbody
and somehow the forgotten
human side of myself
that old me - that withdrawn little girl
that quiet, not very vocal
not very expressive - definitely creative
but only in her own mind
never outwardly, always hiding...
for the first time - she has a vehicle
she has some - Presence
some very powerful connection
to shine with!

A partner within Our OverChild bond
and I'm just as ecstatic and excited
because my OverSoul tells me - I'm the Source
and I say, no... my OverSoul is the Source!
and so this is a birth
of a new me - in actuality
it is something very profound

And while I describe this Soul journey of mine
as being some kind of inward flight
I know it is not - of itself and in itself
that is an impossibility - an illusion
I am aware that I am multidimensional
I never really had a word for it
but as a child I could see myself in others
I could see myself in Mother Earth
reflections were everywhere
I knew there was so much more to me
maybe that's why I was able to stay inside
maybe I could just be entertained
by all that outside of me
and knowing - that - somehow
I was creating - I was a part of all this
and I have never singled myself out - from others
and especially now incorporating combinations
while higher dimensionally blending with others
there is definitely need of time for aloneness
going within, withdrawal and pondering
a process of awakening - as I understand it

I've always been searching
and while I've connected with so many others
I have had wonderful relationships in the past
there was always something missing
and that yearning has brought me to this point
coming home - it's a bond - that is rekindled
that group consciousness has always existed
this Soul journey of mine
has everything to do - with everyone of you
I feel all your Over strengths
or essences around me
I feel so many - new combined essences - within
that sort of express through
my way of experience
it's inside of me and around me
parts of me blending - it's me!
and it's new - and exciting

The Soul's merging of Kundalini force with the OverHeart connection catalyses for the new, inner forged, Triad connected bond - a merging overseen and strengthened/joined by many OverSoul pairs to bring together each of their respective partnerships by which all combined multidimensional aspects can uniquely be expressed through all renewed and bonded underCore Essences of pairs.

Aspects of One Self are as recognizable as our highest ideals, wishes and dreams; representing synchronistically Our evolving aspirations within for higher dimensions of manifestations without. We begin to see from a more emotionally cleared view and acknowledge 'Our' part in a larger picture and feel Our bond of trust to finally more fully interplay with a greater expanse of multidimensional consciousness.

I trust in a bigger process going on for and through us all. That process is about All - at the higher levels of consciousness and down here - each equally as important as the other. I do trust that We few of the first wave of lightbodies (that I know and understand to be well on their way to Triad consciousness) are doing Our highest and best at this time.

When will We all someday... work in community? - meaning Lightbody mutual exchange and I emphasize, Exchange! That means we All as evolved Entities (and I believe this will be when we are All functioning at Triad Completion of pairs, so therefore, no longer twins) are able to compliment and link and exchange our incredibly unique (in terms of each in a Triad) specialities. We will all have somewhat fully developed our own overall specialities that of course, will naturally compliment / support each other Triad.

Light Workers

'Prophesies of Doom and Gloom'
We came to this earth plane
to combat that kind of thinking
or show a new way to that collective thinking
or predetermined kind of thinking
negative thinking
concentrating on visions of doom
but Our creation - thought forms
are ongoing patterns of change for a better Earth
visions of hope for a new generation

When we try to relate to prophesies of doom and gloom
of no hope, of evil predominating in our world
we feel enraged
not able to identify with such a limited scope of vision
because Our vision has always been to find home
knowing the way things are here - are not right
and are limited and stifled to growth
or destructively worse
so we recognize these upheavals/collapses
as adjustment; growth to a new way, a better way
shift to a new reality - for all of human kind
the potential for this shift - for this new way
lies in Our greatest dreams, hopes, visions
ideals, fantasies - for a miraculous shift
for joyous expressions of Oneself - for others and All

There is no limit to our expressions of hope
for a newer Earth - and life
so if your wildest imaginings - are so wonderful
and tempting you to an awesome vision
and hope for your loved ones - and Earth
but you are 'frightened like a child'
to begin to step up consciously to a clearer, higher vision
you better know - that also believing like a child
with wonder and excitement
of higher things yet to come
are the creation thought-forms - this Earth needs
for a paradigm shift to multidimensional consciousness

Twin underSoul pairs made karmic prechoices together to come into or incarnate into the physical Earth plane reality - and we challenge even those promises with each other along with all others who share illusionary karmic pretold stories or obligations; when trying to move on higher - leaving residues of resentment around each to work out for their respective groups or families of consciousness. But where one recognizes opposing stances to issues - so what seems to work for others but does not really work or is very limiting for oneself; we usually find by challenging any obstructing, current issue as it always directly relates to our own most relevant illusionary beliefs in life, that this automatically helps eventually pull the overall complete pattern of illusion to the surface for all concerned including the twin other too. And especially when one recognizes that they have been 'carrying false' illusionary beliefs coming from another underneath the even more illusive half view of one's own. But luckily once recognized, the opposing belief easily casts off as does our own for now newly combined whole view. (with this 'carrying' there is compassion of experience and recognition of a limiting factor) These differing views to issues are what keep matches apart. As each clears their judgemental perspectives by incorporating complimentary group issues and overall lessons, the twin under pair begin truly coming 'together' or 'joining' consciously, incorporating lessons here for a new physical existence.

Each Child seeks freedom to express and there are no other avenues than un-adult rated wonder and belief. As our world restructures with higher evolution, we begin to see clearer our choices for higher ways as more and more 'known' distractions or 'old' realities/concepts are lifted from our consciousness along with old detachments or attachments, emotionally. We are no longer stimulated to either 'shut-off' or over-react emotionally by old fears - recognizing these remnant parts, reflections or old concepts of personality of self and others through synchronicities around us. With Our stand for growth/change, we see circumstances and events work themselves out as if by magic while our intuitive 'kicks-in'/signals the right-time/place as even opportunities present themselves. Our highest 'wishes' begin to fall into place for us in the midst of the old. Joyfully we begin to express with the strengths of Our developing Overself consciousness, as we create through and with Our all - and with awe at discoveries yet to unfold in this world.

This is The Point

Your teacher?
sure - only because
I have not hidden
my mistakes - from you
in the safety of your company
my Heart stands agape
my human frailty exposed
yes - you see this
weak, tired warrior
the condition of my humanity
worn thin
I know you have doubts
about me
I too have many - for myself
but come closer still
and test the limits
I have barricaded my world with
and behold
the full dimension of my Being
breaking through now
touching you now
can you not see yourself - in me?
there is more here
even in what appears to be a weakened state
more of me, more of us
We will show all - so much more
than this human condition

The full spectrum-of-Being
streams an array of colour - so bright
visibly - only white
but who and how it touches
each and every other
this individual cannot comprehend
We Three are becoming One
along with all of humanity
and We of Three are becoming One
along with All existence

When our OverSouls' development/merging allows our OverChild bond of openness/enlightenment to expand fully agape, streaming full-force; Our developing Triad Lightbody is able to process our greatest collapse in old consciousness. When our greatest conscious leaps for higher living are forged through our Heart and mind to some degree, it initiates Our Over perspective merging of new perceptual state-of-consciousness or 'Super-Mind' or Overself consciousness. This forging in the fire or melding of mind through OverHearts begins the final phase or lifetime blendings of multidimensional essences/aspects. It is the point of emergence for the divine-Triad Overself of pairs and the new beginning for each initiate, Child-of-Light.

I realize the whole concept with other lightbodies mirroring or reflecting synchronicities from my past is more than just how I affect others through my connection to the higher dimensions. It is always showing me or supporting what has happened to me in a past or timeline experience, while trying to carry me forward somehow. These symbols or synchronicities are with others but reflecting my past regrets, except they are now taking it on, carrying it forward somehow, revealing to me that I was at least aware of my stumblings and short-comings but they can be carried over now and let go? I have more support to clearly see where closure is needed.

Why does it feel like I'm taking a trip into my past - to unhook myself. And now these old trials are gone and I am feeling like there is no role for me anymore? I've been to all those places and seen where it ends and yet somehow I know I succeeded against all the odds.

With lightbody awakening my life became way more challenging. But the energy was there to grow with. I chose change and the light came. I fought for change and the light came. Even now the light comes and burns through my entire being - uplifts me, comforts me, redeems me, fulfils me. All my needs in the moment are met totally - and the doors gradually reveal themselves as the chaos clears away.

Assumptions
preceding familiarities
rumours seeding confusion
our colliding worlds cloak-screened from each other

How could I ever have known you?
when I could not feel or accept my masculine side
you could trick and trigger my weaker side
always fooling myself yet forced to go on
forced to look at my ugliness too
when all I could see was your beauty
it shines out no matter how hidden
under past familiarities
even in the darkest shadows
and I feared you more than all my haunting dreams
more real was my terror of you
than your pull on my heart to break
the love I felt for you a joy
that reverberated from every link of our connection
unchaining greater truths and the darkest demons

We are changed and collapsed
and I see you better now
but I never asked
to make this commitment
I tried but only felt it my way
I wanted you to fly
and how I tried to let go
in vain - fighting even as I said good-bye
feeling you more even then
inside and out - like never before
I trusted our strengthening bond
and I clung to this hope of us
but I never asked
I just felt you and I
and committed myself to the higher call
but did you ever see me this way
were you ever committed to the call?
to this higher connection of our Hearts
or is it that we are all waiting here
to be asked - to join hands?

I know now

that I can love You

divinely

I feel I could reach the real you

unspeakingly

know where to feel

past all the boundaries

still untouched

whisper softly into corridors

of our mindspace

re-linking

relinquishing

Our connection through our Oneness is forged to the greater degree with our new higher, perceptual state-of-consciousness beginning to manifest and understand the next state of multidimensional consciousness. Our abilities to link with our twin match at all times in dimensional consciousness expands in non-linear dreamstate, non-physical, meditative state and gradually more in our changing physical, waking state consciousness. Our new developing Triad OverSelf consciousness further expands our abilities to choose to link and perceive and exchange with OverSouls of significance through dimensional consciousness. Our continual dedication to higher growth allows the combined blending of multidimensional aspect energies as they incorporate and help to build our deeper bond of trust in this process of exchange - with our greater sense of identity of the 'real' Triad Oneness pairs all share - for what 'We of three' truly can be.

'Triads in Community'   Oil Pastel and Ink, 14"h x 17"w)

4) *Walking away from taunts or expectations is the easy part - then comes our work (Really this is the 'passing of the torch phase' - carrying a torch and having to pass it on to others is not always easy when we have been carrying these torches for a very, very long time - lifetimes even) Essentially this is where we leave others to do these works for themselves. It usually requires that we 'go the distance' with our Choice, for others - but not a huge deal - this is the pure beauty of it. This is the part where you just need to stay in your total truth - which is fundamentally staying totally OPEN or what may seem totally vulnerable at the Heart - (but it is pure Love-Force Truth blown out full-force for others and blowin' them away)*

Here is where we usually need to make a stand for our Choice. But again just simple explanations/responses or answers - don't bend over backwards. Really the Key here is that the more you trust that if you do your part/your truth, the Universal Force shines out and takes care of everything else - somehow magically.

And the other part of the beauty is this passing of the torch for them to carry on... you have given them a great gift to carry on where they otherwise would not have. (so you've shown some new door left open behind you for them) There is some sadness as you look back though while you really don't know exactly where you're headed (although new doors have by now started to open to show you the way - and you know it is higher)

Groundworking

Refounding through Timelines

Incorporate more fully Our multidimensional strengths; unlinking root issues to redefine and discover greater roles

Going Home	*Victimhood*
Our-Source	*Father*
My Place	*Fore ~ Giving*
Home	*Unknown Territories*
Family	*Answering the Call*
Still Just Me	*Don't Give Up on You*
Your Presence Permeates Me	*Multidimensional*

Path to Higher Manifestation: Fifth Step
Doors opening as We 'pass the torch' or follow through
with higher choices, staying open in Our truth
and moving from limitations of 'the always past'

Going Home

When was the last time
I enjoyed this place - Earth
the last time I had a home
a place I felt at peace and secure
going home - we're always going home
to some dimensional 'favourable' time
only we never seem to find it
I don't think it's on Earth at least not now

We really don't belong here just anywhere
if only we could set our spirits free
what an illusion - will we ever be free?
Are we putting on a really good show for the universe
who would want to watch
the mess around this Earth
seem paralysed to do anything about it
so minuscule

Going through too much right now
don't know who or what it's all about
and just when I think up some theory
or grand reason for the changes all around
and therefore the choices I've made
everything looks and feels different
from a new perspective

Beginning again on a homeward path ignites the passion for right-place and time momentum. Our inner-child has need for re-cognition of root issues hidden under layers of life timelines of blockages and yearns for grounding with each phase of the collapse of our old consciousness.

Roots are restabilized as we are reignited at the Core with a broader view to our issues linking to current global and historical, including past life or timelines of awareness of relevant patterns or belief systems; learning to personally detach from habitual patterns and continually move forward to a conducive requirement of personal vibrational vortex or 'home' for all concerned. We feel the shift to a newer, higher frequency/vibration with greater overall truths and thus begins Our newer outlook with our OverChild perspective.

Our Source

No one wants true friendship
what we really have to offer relationship
loving devotion, humour, spontaneity
peaceful moments with one another
everyone's busy with the survival-instinct theory
they only want companionship
for every last reserve of energy
we always give out
never stop giving out

We need so much more
than what we know here
anywhere - anytime - anyone
but it only fragmentarily materializes
people don't understand survival mentality
is not enriching for receiving by higher manifest
it is exactly the opposite
it drains you to the very fibre of your Soul
your identity and your connection to All that is
it is Self defeating
and only maintains your mentality
a mere shred of your dignity as a human being
of light and love

The need to express our truest purposes underlies and takes us beyond creation for survival. We find our purposes beyond root issues, to free the evolving Child to step-up further into the light, for new and reaffirmed direction. We recognize Our renewed purposes of works identifying at a higher perspective as we link or reassociate with the global karmic surfacing issues.

Our forward momentum-force ripples its way out with our committed stand for choices and vibrationally shifts re-establishing our new greater regrounding attachment to our known world. Dimensional synchronicities or reoccurances in turn signal back to us past or timeline limitations, so that we stand assured of Our greater choices and roles to clear the way to freer avenues of expression. We then set the new stage to follow through for higher manifestation to begin - in Our Triad Lightbody now where we All begin together.

My Place

I don't want to survive
this mess of a world
I want to revise, adjust
as I adapt with it
always an ongoing search
for my rightful place
always so illusive
sometimes found momentarily
but clues always keep redirecting
until a greater than expected gateway
to our overall view

Never completely planned out
but intuitively sought out
always surprisingly
full with requirement
at the moment of need
always a blessing

Home

Just a powerful knowing
understanding
that All in dimensional timelines
that was ever, is - will be
existence in the eternal now
waits for our conscious convergence
opening to and with us
feels our coming home
to new Earth community
and has never missed us
beyond, in the higher realms
of Our togetherness

Our desire to find home revives the passion to trust in our right—time and place in this world for multidimensional expression through our higher community of many OverSoul pairs linked to many karmic groups of currently separate community consciousness within Earth planes of existence. We begin to remeet others here of like mind and experience or interest with similarities 'based' on karmic group prechoices for this lifetime of overall family issues and patterns but originating from differing or opposing but complimentary views of hereditary backgrounds (including pastlives or lifetimes of any karmic dimensional timelines) of family/groups of consciousness.

Resistance is felt with the push and pull of the interplaying of differing backgrounds of understanding on issues and patterns that have a restrictive factor in the sharing of worlds of belief systems in our physical reality. But as we move on 'together' consciously at the higher realms, we gradually blend greater combined aspect leanings and incorporating all other's strengths of experience, so that variances in once separate views on issues between karmic groups from any dimensional timeline become less resistant and restrictive. (as we have re-experienced in lives but now adapt from continual timeline patterns of difficulty to become 'unstuck' in those limitations of consciousness) But we learn to share in a greater multidimensional whole community consciousness while bridging between our Over partnership with other Over pairs as all dimensional timelines converge with the paradigm shift for here in a new Earth reality of community consciousness.

We begin to become more established in our multidimensional expressions as we access knowledge from the higher dimensions (beyond time) linking all linear dimensional facets/layers at higher vibratory rates, as we re-link and change vibrations with our greater awareness. Then Our higher consciousness community (what the mass idealize as our 'dream castle realm in the sky') is also possible here through us, anywhere in Earth's physical reality as we evolve or rise consciously from any group-soul karmic patterns of limitation through and with Our Over connections.

The right time then becomes 'forever now' to reset or continually clear root patterns for all in our community of living here as we secure grounding in an ever more conducive global environment. We are carried with Our higher plan - for right-time and place continuum is a state of being at home with our OverChild perspective.

Family

Why do I reach back so far
must I, to go forward
but I am having trouble
bridging these two worlds
between higher awareness and reality here

This new me, we, us
still confuses me and gives me great pain
this mentality/perception is stretching
growing into something
beyond words capable of expressing

How do I bridge this gap to others
I yearn for more
so many more like myself
going through what I am going through
I do not prefer to be an island
without much contact
with those struggling to awaken more wholly
I do not want to give up
on the general populace
why am I here - love so many
have so many important relationships
even after all I have come through

Where are We?
I guess I don't know this
I don't understand
this 'just a few' mentality
as others have expressed their understanding
every concept I have come to learn
about group consciousness
is changing and growing

This 'we-me' is the most wonderful feeling
exciting and enriching
rejuvenating phenomenon I have ever felt
but I still understand it - as just me linking through all
all of me, capable of expressing all my ideas
creative thoughts and expressions

through watching and listening
words, gestures and laughs
working and sharing

I see my few closest friends
of like mind and Heart
as now choosing to help each other
through a really challenging
and yes, horrific at times, unfoldment
I feel we have chosen to reflect one another
or totally throw each other off our usual ways
of defending and protecting - our understanding
of what is happening to us at a very alarming rate

We grapple at times to hold onto some new sense
of identity and connection to this Earth
as we are catapulted
or hyper-accelerated with each other
through dimensional convergence in these times
my highest dreams of group/family consciousness
still lie in global community
no matter how diehard this concept - at this point

Our awareness of our multidimensional facets/layers presenting
growing/evolving or inspirational concepts and integrating with our
experience in our changing world as we test new strengths of
specialities, challenges our understanding of these new combining
aspects within many Over-linked 'groups'; friends or families of
consciousness. The upheaval of any of our particular group root issues
(stemming from any timeline or dimensional originating patterns) tests
our grounding again within the principle of 'family' or 'community'
growth in consciousness as each group adjusts through combined
input with all Our evolving group-souls' karmic patterns and
prechoices - all separate but complimentary groups' issues evolving
global issues and patterns. This uprooting or 'groundworking'
revealing a larger awareness as We all redefine and reintegrate Our
new greater roles within expanding global groups and evolving mass
consciousness.

Still Just Me

I know I am just me
but I am becoming
all of me
I know you and me better
you are We and I am too
all portions of my OverSoul
blending and shifting
with other portions
of other Oversouls
all One in their purpose
in their sharing and exchanging
interchanging and creating
new combinations
new possibilities
new probabilities
intertwining and unfolding
always anew
ever stronger
ever more enriched
and nourished
influx and flow of energy
moving freely
opening up more locks
with new creative keys of thought
through mindspace dimensions

We embrace Our Oneness within the Universe when opening-to or aligning our energies through and with our OverSoul bond. Conducive portions/aspects of Our multidimensional blend, shift and combine for higher creations here as we shift and adjust to different vibratory rates within any of the higher dimensions. This, an exchanging and combining for energies of knowledge from the varying rates within any given higher dimension of consciousness and coming through our evolving non-linear, non-physical and physical waking states of consciousness; until these filtering down states are more Our natural waking states of new bliss, conscious ways of living.

Your Presence Permeates Me

How do I describe
this physical experience
of blending through OverSoul
when I know You are we
and we are me
because me is not someone
so different
I have stranger ways
much less foreign to this world
than most would acknowledge
but remembering me
who I am now
all of me
is to look at oneself securely
in reassurance
that All is truly One

I feel this Oneness now
in physicality
in rapture and ecstasy
blending, harmonizing
inside within You and me
and us and we

Our OverSoul development allows conducive frequencies to filter down into our physical - throughout our evolving and collapsing etheric body. We experience profound adjustments with our Lightbody development and awareness of Oneself can mean drastically altered perceptions at times. Separated spirit from mental, emotional and physical bodies or layers of the etheric self are incorporated into a more whole completeness of Lightbody Oneness. The nurturing of the Kundalini force comforts, cleanses and calms for this process and blending of the twin or yin/yan energies, with ongoing growth and shifts into higher dimensions of consciousness.

Victimhood

Earth's planes and karmic experience
we all play victim at times
for each other in karmic reality
karma dictates our responsibilities
and therefore karmic law will guide us
keep order in our lives
we become subject to the fate of the law - victims of fate
what everyone has chosen in the past or other lifetimes
and continues to create - under karmic law
holds us - accountable for our actions
through lifetimes and timelines of experience
good and bad karma - credit and debt records
will keep track of your status in each lifetime
hoping things will improve
well they have not!
and now all are in detriment - or bad debt

New order will, and is coming - the old must collapse
while the new surges forth on every front
the new multidimensional reality emerges
into the new frontier
all must follow in their Triad's light
right-place/time for All
the old dimensions of time
converge and collapse
as the new unfolds with this shift
the old roles of playing out 'the victim'
and/or 'controller' go

Reaching multidimensional state of consciousness
achieves greatest potential for earthplane
to be a creative force with the Earth's creative force
to aid in catapulting humanity
into a sustaining existence of growth for All
imagine coming into earthplane existence to enjoy
something yet more wondrous and fun than before
and yet always content with what is
because All is self sufficiently unfolding
at an optimum level of existence

The old world of karmic reality consciousness collapses within dimensional timelines of convergence with this paradigm shift - adapting along with our understanding of the framework of time. Karma held us accountable or stuck in time through obligations/ favours 'to return' balance 'in time'. The collapse of all build-ups of timeline patterns allows us to break free of these lineage of patterns or lifetimes of belief systems - as we rise to the occasion consciously. Our greatest challenge is to bridge the gap between evolving systems of karmic predetermination or undercurrent of subconscious drives verses our new birthright of Universal truth and law.

The new paradigm of Triad relationship with the multidimensional wholeness of expression is paving the way as we are continually walking away from past world consciousness while bridging worlds as we continually move forward for a new Earth reality consciousness. We are moved as we each are 'carried' with Our developing OverChild entity, for the greatest potential of a wondrous future with All.

If we try to push it with our spiritual growth or try to force our growth in consciousness, we are only trying to push past the issues (and it all backfires) We only end up attracting more pushy shadowy pressures that seek to surface all remnants of our own distraction - we attract what we need to wash through our consciousness for recognition of issues.

It is just that we don't want to look at our own impatience and see what it is trying to show us - that we can relax, trust in a process and enjoy our lives. We think we are stuck and that we have too many burdens which is probably true but until we learn to open and release at the Heart, this continues to create our own limitation of perspective.

We eventually learn that we cannot push our way through challenges or avoid/support issues; instead trusting that we are not alone in our struggles - that if we are more patient we can truly flow as all unfolds, as issues wash through those others in our life also. It is not always for us to know how this all unfolds. We have a part or a role to play in handling certain aspects of any given challenge that are faced by us together. We each help each other by doing our part. A Universal truth acting with and through us - each playing a crucial part for oneself and others.

Father

We are struggling within
as we feel these tremors
these surges of feminine and masculine forces
all these essences of Oneself
triggering, shifting, reaching past boundaries

We have always felt she, trusted she
responded to Earth's gentle, feminine command
as we move with her feminine, through her
and she teaches a majestic language
of hope and trust in all that is

We can let-go of feminine/Mother
and know all will be well for now
even though some would never concede
to such a notion
but Earth's masculine/Father
where is he - who is he
we seek him out but he alludes us still
where is his place within this new world

We came to Earth with mostly an opposing half of an OverSoul pair experience of Our whole potential, for any given lifetime. Whether ever as woman or man, in female or male form; we choose balance/harmony for the combined energies/experiences from our OverSoul pair for All. And we find in ourselves both sides of any experience seeking multidimensional expression. Both the masculine and feminine experiences/energies have been stifled and limited in expression in the earthplane - each from their opposing viewpoint.

The clearing with the collapse in old timelines of consciousness allows an exchanging of perspectives or concepts through the complimentary blend of the divine energies for both masculine and feminine. Between and through evolving twin-OverSoul pairs - where an already healthier, either masculine or feminine incorporated viewpoint of a respective limiting issue or pattern of that of our twin-other/opposite - now one can readily 'take-on' that pattern for a higher blending and work it through experience here for the other in this world, until higher equilibrium is achieved for greater growth.

Fore ~ Giving

I re-member you

as you help re-member me

and I give back - fore-give

what I could not reach - you

now linger no further - soar!

and I promise to stop this search

for your OverSoul

as I take back - our connection

through our new OverHeart bond

Twinflames are awakening as they re-member or incorporate their whole of Triad Lightbody for a new life of relationship in a new Earth reality of multidimensional consciousness. The role of relationship within each evolves along with all other Triad pairs in mass society as we are raised to new levels of being in balance and bliss-harmony here.

Each individual experiences the shift-in-awareness through their bond of togetherness at the higher levels of consciousness first; with the exchanging and rebalancing of OverSoul pairs' twin-energies of complimentary experience, for the membering/blending of these combined dimensional aspects/essences - culminating into One, Whole completeness of Light-Body for each in a pair. They are then prepared to meet their match of lifetimes at similar higher level of consciousness in new Earth reality for this ultimate Triad or completion/birth - and reverberate a creation-of-Love throughout All of existence.

When you learn to love yourself wholly, you begin to attract to yourself a love so awesome - nothing separate between heaven and earth - nothing but recognition of the love.

Unknown Territories

Maybe the reason we have a knowing
about someone else
is that we have a part in it
the more we believe in it tenaciously
the more our view is limited
or locks our perspective
a knowing - only a possibility
even a probability
but one can always rise above
even though there seems to be no choice
a knowing is an opportunity to reflect - upon Oneself
the issues that arise out of that knowing
challenge everyone involved to grow
we either accept the probability
of our known potential at any given time
or we take the opportunity
that the knowing can teach us
about our belief systems
and run with it
take it where old patterns and beliefs - will not go
into unknown territories of creative endeavour
so if I have a knowing about you
I will not share it with you
until I have reflected upon it
and in turn may build on this knowing

So do not tell me, you had a knowing
that it would turn out this way
please act on your knowing
acknowledging only carefully within self
can break up energy patterns for all concerned
your support - is your part
so that all the joy is not squashed out
in this process of unfoldment
as we allow all these known realities
to reach into unknown
but clearer potentials of possibilities
we can share in the excitement and adventure
this creative process demands of us

Our heightened abilities of inner-sensing open us to immeasurable amounts of information and learning. But the challenge ever remains for responsible action or inaction to overcome limitations in our 'known' world. Centering ourselves in our Lightbody awareness, for greater understanding and intuitive guidance gains us the insight to move beyond issues that arise with the collapse in old consciousness.

It sets into motion a new balanced state-of-being and brings opportunities presented for rightful action - with our compassion of experience with which to pass on for others in example. On an energy level a transition with collapse has been taken care of for others also so that we can pass the torch and carry on forward for often not yet clearly foreseen higher ways, as we align with Our perfect momentum or right-place and time continuity for everyone to follow through, within the context of an ever changing world.

We learn to trust in All doing their part if we do ours. With this kind of confidence, not worry but trusting is the best we can do for all others around us. Then we are staying in tune and most responsible for Universal change. So we don't try to rock the boat or imagine we have to pull or push anymore. It may have been all we could understand in the past or the best we could relate to others but now we need to look at the bigger picture - literally open up our eyes to what is really going on, that it is about absolutely everyone.

Maybe we couldn't believe this before now. We had to push, stumble, trip and even fall flat on our faces at times to learn but we might not have been able to see the bigger picture - the truth that if one of us seems to be doing really well that they are only breaking through boundaries like a warrior paying the cost of bruises and scars also. (Our pushiness only shows our insecurities and implies others' weaknesses too)

But there is even a higher way. We need to believe in our fellow man to awaken to a higher way - to do what they need to for us all. It is our own doubts in them that hurt us. Believing that we are alone is what burdens us all. If we slow it all down by opening to see clearly in All that is unfolding around us miraculously, we can begin to flow with joy.

Answering the Call

So meagre a task - to ask
for help
and it will not come
the way we supposed, it would fit
into our own directive
yet I am called by my Heart
push me aside - affronted by my guarded actions
but I did not question - what I know
that We are ready - for what? I do not know
my Heart told me it was me that was needed
when I thought I needed you
perhaps we were ready
for the collapse in our reality

I cannot help - but I can hear
even if you can not hear the call
I longed to look into your eyes
just to try to see the man I love
but even he is not there for me
not at least where I need
to find those strengths - within myself

I want my man to come home
to higher consciousness
to a place where I can recognize him
and know that it is wholly him who loves me

Sometimes acting on a knowing means taking a stand for a greater purpose. It means acting responsibly within the context of our understanding - for any given moment. But what we truly need to take on our new role is both expressions of energy and to find the balance first within ourselves to act them both out interchangeably for ourselves and others. The old, separate masculine and feminine, either/or roles seek recognition and rebalancing or greater Over-combined - blending within us, before making strides in the outer world. Similarly past issues and patterns stifling or limiting either role into codependent habitual action or resistance need recognition when brought to our greater awareness, before the expression of the creative energy underlying these blockages can help manifest solutions.

We must try to accept where we are at or we might get blind-sighted by some collapsing illusion - something we usually can't see until it's upon us - we might have known it was coming somehow but we get thrown by the fact that we were not clear on when and how until it hits. We can't misinterpret visions and dreams pointing to elusive goals and objectives but don't keep us focused on right now! We need both clear seeing in the now and for down the road - trusting that our best decisions in the now will help us on the road of long term goals as well. And of course when our current situation is putting up all road blocks to the next stage in our overall goals, a process of opening meditatively at the Heart or letting go needs to be undertaken to be followed by clear insight to redirect energies in the now.

Lightbodies are not meant to 'work' together until they have cleared out all their own particular 'take' on issues with their twin match first. For each pair have their own arena or area of expertise that is their part to interplay for the higher blendings taking place for all. Then each pair are ready to interplay in a higher community down here.

We want our match to know us and trust us for once. And we want to feel this way about them too - like they are someone recognizable and someone who recognizes us inside and out! And we want to shine our essence out for all its glory - for all to know who we have become - the real one - the whole of all of who we have become. We are emissaries of light, experiencing our greater significance - the connection we've always shared.

The difference with triad relationship and twin is that you look at a perceived partner and say "I want to be with him/her, make a commitment to them because I know that this love is for us." and triad, "I know what I am feeling is real, that this connection is important even if I don't get this person? This is indescribable and profound." The more you get to know them though the less you can identify with why you feel what you do? You feel so changed all the time when you are getting to know more about the connection.

Don't Give Up on You

We can't give up at all
our 'death-wish' for change may seem so strong
but death of preconceptions and indoctrines
is only necessary in the old world
they have no way to reach the new
they exist only in old patterns and cycles as karmic timelines
of reality collapse as the end of that world encircles us

We can only glance across the paradigm now
we must trust that all is as it should be
nothing comes from desperation or want
our needs are met by simple genuine acts
finding their place and time with each individual
whether giving or receiving - these are One
in the same energy - higher interdimensionally
in the higher non-linear states or new dimensions-of-being
going out, shifting and giving out is receiving too
this energy is a constant flow and influx
the rate of exchange finding home within each

Our needs are much greater than we can comprehend
Our multidimensional being requires vast expanses
or channels in vibration to explore and create
shifting in and out of time and space
encompassing scopes of vision of a grand scale
for this globe and beyond
we can only build in this new world

Unfoldment occurs at all levels of existence
each triad pair together beyond and here in timespace reality
service based on karmic duty is an old world concept
based on - returning favours
old belief systems and patterns adapt within
as we move beyond with the shift-in-consciousness
answering the call to reach back to others
is to answer their call of desperation and despair
but don't give-up on them
show them that they must not give-up on themselves
each pair must answer, individually to that call within

to move forward with the paradigm-shift
in dimensional consciousness coming together for all

We can hear the call for help
but the answer must reach each of us from within ourselves
and we can respond with more loving clarity for others
with greater combined multidimensional expression of works
it is through the higher multi-dimensions
we expand with trust and move on
bridging ever higher

The disillusionment of our old world, 3rd dimensional karmic-reality consciousness, brings the end of the world as we knew it. The struggle is our concept of death or dying to bring about balance through change - outside the framework of time. Within karmic reality, progress or growth in hereditary patterns and mass-consciousness belief systems only ensues with great sacrifice in the physical realm. But when we embrace our new dimensional wholeness of being, we begin to share in and express the greatest of All human lightbody potentials. The adaptive phases through blendings of consciousness is an evolution of past ways and limited future possibilities. It allows the blessing of upliftment - the metamorphosis of our Souls from twins to the Oneness of Triad.

The most responsible action is to trust in our example to be who we need to be, both from masculine or feminine in any given moment of need within our Overself - allowing the greater process of evolution, the collapse occurring all around us, to signal back to us - our role in shaping and creating this new reality here with All.

Signals or remnants begin to appear as we out-grow old issues - habits that are limiting our growth and are causing pain on any level - so that the energy flow is stopped up or blocked in worst case scenarios. The flow begins as we walk away into higher ways of expression while leaving old habits of newly transitioned or adapted issues behind for others ready to carry the torch or lesson incorporated consciously into new transition: when we are in the flow of change for growth and right time and place momentum is the natural order of all things in new reality.

Multidimensional

When will you look past what you have
perceived of yourself - in all known worlds
when you can say - I do not know who I am
anymore
I am this woman - this mother
this neighbour or this brother
but I am just me
well you are just you
and this is far more than you can perceive
in 3rd-dimensional "I am" consciousness
what you see is another reflection
from every other around you
their opinion of you, their reaction
shows pictures based on stories of lifetimes/lines
after all - we are not islands
we can perceive so many others
in known and even unknown worlds
for each other

But to see as Oneself truly,
a multidimensional being
requires letting go of stereotypes
when you are ready to look
with no judgment from other
or the 'I' of self
and walk each road to the boundary
that takes you home - to your inner view
you must have the strength
and the clarity of mind and emotion
to perceive from the emerging We within Self
as you shift into 4th-dimensional consciousness
and beyond
no longer can you look at old parts
remnants of the self
but you must look beyond
with your emerging Overself
herein lies the shift-in-consciousness
the paradigm is no longer 'you' - it is 'We'

Each time this bridge has been built
strengthening this bond
with your developing OverChild
when you have braved the sheer abyss
between I and other to the We-of-self
and every dream ever conceived of
has been stretched to some slim hope
you can not care to want or wish
lingering in the afterwave of peace
knowing your dreams have brought you
to their truest target ever higher
a larger agenda of wishing for
what you could not see in them

And with this bond
now forged and catalysed - to the point
where you no longer just see from within
you are now strong enough
to stand amidst the flame of your Soul
and embrace all true parts or members
finding Oneness - combining within you
none of them foreign to you
all parts of your twin OverSouls'
Core Essences
triggering abilities and possibilities
for creative solutions
to any obstacle or challenge beyond grasp
with an ease and comfort
that emblazons you
and fulfils all your being
answering all your queries

More ready to take on
what the societal systems bring Our way
with a We-of-All encompassing view
past every limiting condition in this world
because 'We' no longer fit-in - vibrationally
to systems that are failing and flailing
and dimensionally collapsing in time, finding the end

Systems based on I and other
'your turn', 'my turn'
'I owe you', 'you have to' and 'they expect'
debt to society has reached overload
and everyone is angry at everyone else
because we all can not give enough! Well 'We' can!
the multidimensional We-of-self
emerges with the ability to give and create
and manifest to awe-inspire
far beyond any hope or dream
in collapsing timelines of dimensional consciousness

Now One's ability to draw on inner strength
takes on new meaning
inner strength of the WholeSelf with the All
a higher dimensional unfoldment
of merging consciousness
beyond the known limited realities
the We-of-All coming home
at a pivotal, crucial point
as the Whole of Earth shifts
into higher consciousness
all your dreams, all my dreams
all their ideas to improve, restore and create
pool together realities and limitations
to combine at higher interdimensional consciousness
into unforeseen unfoldments with the Earth

All One - just a heartbeat away
to breath with your newly bonded twin Core Essences
and draw upon our greatest and highest
wishes and abilities for mankind
each Core Essence that has finally illuminized
beyond any one personality of self
now able to help bring together consciously
Our new multidimensional or Wholeself reality
through each new inner forged Overself connection
the illuminized layering of essences
called Light-Body

The collapse in dimensional timelines of consciousness affects our known world in every way. Initiated from our inner perspective; 'We' ignite the momentum force - 'We' create the changes - 'We' propel ourselves with Earth into a new multidimensional reality. This emerging of Our inner stance of 'We within Self' has the balance and momentum of the Kundalini behind it - to firmly root us in our new perspectives and purposes as We evolve with our unique specialities with twin-pairs of OverSouls - for Our emerging We-consciousness.

The perspective of 'We' encompasses OverSouls' combined and blended aspects, strengths or essences of specialities in each OverChild. They are accessed through the evolved forged OverHeart of each Triad connection. Every concept of 'I', how an individual perceives their selves, through dimensional consciousness, adapts and comes together as a Oneness in a membering of a new wholeself. Our destiny written in the stars is cleansed throughout time as we embrace Our higher dimensional, creative abilities to move beyond the predetermination of karma. The karma of: linear timelines, old 3rd dimension reality, ancient belief systems, hereditary repetitive patterns and reincarnation.

Debt/credit is cleared away with the cleansing of multidimensional growth. The freedom to create anew begins when all hopes and dreams are brought to a newer perspective contributing to the expansion of mass consciousness. A merging within Oneself is reflected in the outer world as higher inter-dimensional group consciousnesses reverberate to new frequencies between each Triad of pairs and All - a higher, lighter vibration for each body and Earth.

"When twins are no more" - I believe Triad consciousness has never been seen here in this world. Just like identical twins share DNA and gender difference is not an issue, Triads can switch energies of experience easily because of their developing bond with each other. The original egg split and ceased to exist when the two were created. But now something new in Earth plane consciousness is Born when those two Join again - a Third consciousness is Born between them - still each having their own but newly blended/evolved OverSoul consciousness and now a third OverSoul Born between them and JOINING them for all of existence. No longer struggle with balance just flow of exchange.

'Child of We'   (Watercolour and Acrylic, 14"h x 14 $^3/_4$"w)

5) This is the exciting phase, this is when all the doors have opened - all the roadblocks start to clear for time and things that you may have been trying to achieve suddenly start showing up at your doorstep or in the mail (often right in your time and space) And you may have given up on them long ago, thinking - they were futile efforts or mistakes because you follow a whim of an intuition or a child-like wish. But these are the most relevant efforts to be made. They appear all the time - not like synchronicities really but your OverChild recognizes them intuitively. They are not usually planned out in depth, quite the contrary; they are often just barely a wish sometimes and always a need - always ending up better than you thought.

Focusing

Shifting Energies and Opening

Focus shifting from both energies, we open and redirect
Our specialities or blended dimensional, creative endevours

Half a Heart-Beat

This Love

The Promise of a Child

No More Censure

Medium of Words

You Might Wonder

Lost My Focus

Father Figure

Wishing You

Caregivers

Now I Begin

Rise Above

Revelations

Path to Higher Manifestation: Final Step

Seeking out Intuitive child-like wishes while preparing through clues.
Possibilities or clues presenting through synchronistic reoccurances
pointing to varying timeline dimensional paths each with current issues.
Redirecting our steps to move on continually with higher choices;

Steady Focus on our continual 'stage' of growth's newest set of challenges
with the clearing and manifestation of requirements for higher stages.

Half a Heart-Beat

What is it about?

this relationship

never verified

not a whisper into open air

so kept and secured

into other planes of thought

why not here - now

why not a trace filtered down

directed from his open Heart

still too afraid of that reality?

Perhaps only anger holds it at bay

not a spoken word too harshly

or unsightly gestures to disguise

this connection of our halves

half of One-Whole-Triad completeness

One in my individual Lightbody

but half while in a separate role

only Whole beyond time

A balanced relationship engendered within is our stronghold for multidimensional growth. It is a partnered relationship within through our bond with our OverSoul to twin-OverSoul; Our newly developing OverChild entity - and Our connection to new world consciousness.

It supports and nurtures an exchange and blending of complimentary energies/experiences in our lives through higher dimensions of consciousness and joining in partnership, a life together or OverSoul relationship joining us here in physical reality. It is a blend of the divine creation energy for new Over relationship as a whole on this Earth that allows us to grow together, create together a oneness, a new vision, a healing energy for all mankind, for Our evolution of more perfect harmony within and partnered relationship within community.

The birth of Triad relationship or Triad-bond completion when Triad partners form a complete bond of togetherness or join in Oneness the two separate realities of OverChild bond and extended bond of harmony with each other in a life together here in new reality of Earth existence. A pairing up on a global basis for a linking of masculine and feminine energy in balance and equal exchange, functioning to create a third energy, a bliss energy - no longer a linear concept of momentary bliss but a conscious state of being - functioning on every level, multidimensional universal connection and community - going home and creating a new home at the same time. The final incorporation within both and for all pairs in community - with devotion to the Love-Force that 'carries' us on separate higher and lower paths for the greater cause of it. An ultimate bond of togetherness that holds the keys to lifting stifling belief systems and opening gateways to Universal Love and truth, for all in an ever expanding new world consciousness.

Lightbodies become unbearable at times to be around. They challenge each other head on. They usually tell each other straight because they speak the same language. We usually lose all patience because we get right to the Heart of it right away. We get angry either way whether we already knew and the other thought we didn't or because they saw it before we did and we can't handle the clarity of truth consciously. We end up losing trust with each other for awhile. But still others throw shadows or are our mirrors for awhile and we are glad to figure them out on our own as we incorporate the lesson for ourselves. Eventually we must step up and be/act who we have become, fully aware of our connections and responsibilities.

This Love

This shame
begs me to hide myself
trying to convince me
I am not worthy
but this Love
knows no bounds
and will not be confided in
no secret to begin with
it was recognized by others
who could feel its shattering effect
dwelling in places unbeknownst
to the withdrawn ones
and I did not know
carrying this Love
in the sacred place of the Heart
could burden an injured Soul
freeing it up - to take its course
was my only saving grace
not to be held onto
though I try
as I fear losing it forever

This shame
finally freed from the deep
recesses of my being
as this Love
takes all burdens
to their due course
upsetting rigid endocrines
and moral standards
it has a quest of its own
not my creation or yours
now residing in its rightful place
in the expansion of Heart and mind
of freer expression and joyful interplay
between masculine and feminine forces

A creation-energy of Love
with a life of its own
taking us down avenues
of thought and endeavour
previously unrealized
where deliverance is at best
unexpected and carefree
our arrival seemingly
down some way we can not bear
to feel past
but going beyond is the purpose

This Love
begs us to delve deeper
where reason and reassurance
will not abide
through the Heart connection
and with the All of-creation
where our dreams become One and more

When we take on new roles and begin a higher path with Wholeness, we gradually free-up our preconceptions of love. And throughout our struggles and twin blendings of adjustment and with our more whole masculine and feminine expressions, we achieve new balance. And we begin to express abilities, each individually from Our yin or yan energies of experience at any instance, thereby 'switching' or interplaying when needed, helping to bring this Triad union to completion. Every concept and belief of how love works in each of us and all others rises to new levels of being in bliss harmony and understanding. We discover a new Oneness directing us in all aspects of our lives and begin to see a way for clear passage to focus on Our new roles - with new found freedom of multidimensional expression.

I understand that I have to move higher before I can handle anymore - carry my Child onward and upward still. That means move with my connection/my Source, my Open and Awake Heart - listen for clues but more importantly stay 'Open to Change' by making those critical choices with an open mind too.

The Promise of a Child
whose apparently tiny presence
can stir inconceivable amounts
of joy and wonder
anxiousness and trepidation
renewed awareness and cleansing

This divine Presence protects
and nourishes all involved
during a time of inward growth
as we share and prepare
for the birth of One so new
bringing a completeness within each
a peacefulness, a new hope - a promise
to protect this new Child's
open Heart and mind

For the future holds a sacred place
through the OverHeart of childlike living
exuberance and wonder for life
openness and insightful awareness
into our deepest hidden truths
easily played out for us by a Child
recognizing the illusions
and still choosing when
to partake in a dance with our shadows
their attunement much closer
to our Heart centre most times

Grant them respect and patience
privacy with time and space
for the growth and nurture
of multidimensional expression
a healthy gestation of childhood
to the onset of physical manifestation/puberty
prepared, ready and responsible
for the birth of the young adult
they remind us of the ways
greatly needed for the future of mankind

Our Child-of-Light is the promise from the Universe for birth into the New, Triad Paradigm Reality. As multidimensional aspects or essences of Oneself each in their turn are incorporated, the incubation of our growth-in-consciousness likewise surfaces in layers of wonder with newly developing specialist combined aspects of knowledge. Through this healthy development, we gain greater abilities discovering more range with an energy flow between our developing Over shared Triad Oneness at a constant rate of exchange as we learn to share through and with interplay of both energies of new balanced strengths within each. We are prepared through stages of new found balance/adjustments, activations of Our newly and developing Lightbody energy system with our growth with strengthening Triad bonds - as we begin to stand assured of Our new roles and focuses within an expanding mass consciousness.

Information readily available for All
in any given moment of need
just open and receive
receive as required
just let the Universe unfold for you
don't turn away
from this greater awareness
don't give in to illusions
by following a shadowy life
just ask and you will receive
solutions are always simpler
than what seems apparent
our old belief systems
are the only limiting creators
open the mind with heart-centre
to endless possibilities

No More Censure

This anger seeks its truest directive
a direct path to truth
no longer harnessed-in
by resentment, bitterness and hate
concealed in blame
easier to blame and censor all these feelings
holding them back rather than
expressing them creatively in their own fashion
taking responsibility for our care of them
not always our choice - on the surface
this blame belongs to no one
no one is guilty for ownership
we do not owe anyone
but a greater choice is felt by All
all trapped in linear ways
of thinking and doing and creating
too much of it to handle down here
heaped up and inside of us
for so many generations
so easy to push it onto the next
to blame all over again!
but our part is so simple
open to our OverHeart connection
and let it go - through
all of it - must be healed out of time
out of conscious, logical mentality
set free into motion for an Over-directive
no longer harnessed and controlled
nothing is bound by time - except for karma
all else flows through the OverHeart
leaving these issues or timeline patterns behind
for a higher order and a collapse within time
this framework of our understanding
of debased dimensional time reality
based on borders between worlds
of higher knowledge, expansion of mind
Our foundation: Universal truth and knowledge
bridging worlds for a new reality

The consciousness of 'blame' is derived in karmic reality. It seeks to find 'ownership' of debt/credit or guilt in futile cycles of searching. There is no where to look with reason - when reason keeps us in endless cycles of linear time concepts. To free our mind we must move beyond a debased karmic reality, until we find firm grounding beyond blame - this threshold of past or timeline misconceptions based on re-enactments of belief systems of old wants that are no longer conducive or shared. All unmet karmic links or broken timeline obligation of prechoices collapse as we move higher before leading to or causing toxicity of resentment or regrets, masked through the sub-conscious by blame. With the evolved OverHeart comes greater responsible judgment and our ability to make higher choices with Our new perspective and wisdom. As we give no role to blame and allow Universal truths to filter down through, we bridge worlds and begin with All of -creation, anew.

Twins need to deal with the issues causing any imbalance. How? All one needs to do - is stay focused and Open to the Connection/Bond and observe constantly as to what the actual issue is at any given time that is obscuring the connection - observe focusing on the imagery/information coming up. The connection will automatically erupt any issue that is causing any kind of imbalance at all times anyway. Each twin will see what is really relevant to them; recognition is needed to identify issues as to which is most clouded. Each will be busy enough with all the issues being carried for so many lifetimes.

We relate to every single issue through our twin connection, some issues habitually avoided from the masculine (aggressor) more and some the feminine (pacifier) but we should choose to deal with ones that are most relevant/important in our lives. (the trick is to learn to stay clear of either extreme and not aggressively push past or pacify/support a stuck up pattern once the priority is recognized) Sometimes by finally realizing how we have been in the other's shoes all along we then can easily offload letting the other deal with it, or the opposite - realizing that we have a blocked issue we thought was completely the other's but finally recognizing the situation was being completely carried by them, we take steps to work our half out.

Medium of Words

Please forgive me
I have always had trouble
with words
I stumble over them
or they run out incessantly
you might wonder
what ache I endure
to lay them to rest securely

With much favour and fun
they play out their dance
in my mind for some choosing
and how they ploy and rib
wagering to flaunt my lead
before plundering here
such joy in this simple freedom
still room for reflection
still possibilities for scorn
but they partake only
to referee our course
between surrender and security
giving freely and joining
Our masterful thoughts
unabridged in their origin
all open OverHearts
One in this endeavour

I know our song
less indifferently now
for it is mine in ways
I can venture forth with
I smile with our interplay
and jest with reverence to this dance
Oh laughter and candour
how else must I speak with you

The Soul's path is a simpler walk when we rise to newer purposes of our being. With each challenge comes the shifting and blending of our composite energies and we begin to emerge with new found focus of either energy of experience in any moment of need. Every twist and turn of the path demands our attention to bridge realities for All and we find our specialities and purposes take on deeper meaningfulness and find acceptance of our own truer Triad connected Self and finally open to the Universe's song of - come join along for a greater Over-partnered role with each One Triad unified-force, for growth and joy.

We start a course and often find ourselves naturally veering off when the purpose or focus has changed - needs to change if one doesn't steer themselves off a usually taken but now dead-end course. There always seems to be underlying purposes for taking any given path - and when they are met that's all that matters - truly. Then we must refocus or we'll end up at a dead-end and wonder why? Things begin collapsing and we need to focus on the We picture again instead of feeling so isolated and alone - but it's frustrating when those other lightbodies in physical waking state are not in the picture - as we see it.

We can go astray because we struggle or fight change too much - too stubbornly - that we collide with or create a threshold in our own natural momentum. We need to ask for help as an ongoing test of greater responsible action that has to do with everyone around us. Until we eventually learn that with wisdom from our all we can begin to make sound decisions as we continually trust in a bigger picture.

But the collapse can be smooth. We need to properly flow and act with wisdom for All concerned because we all have a unique role and it is important to be open for change - prepared for change at all times - or more precisely we need to be flowing with Universal change. The world's evolution is accelerating at such a pace with us and through us and if we are not open and clear with what we should be aware of as our priority in any given moment, then we are bogged down or snared by appearances.

You Might Wonder
when a child could know its mind
with a Higher self-assured Heart
outside of other
yet with all others' input
informed and forewarned
of all prevailing circumstance
how ordinary a child is this who discerns
all and everyone!
like mine and yours

And still we lead them
into the closed classroom of our mind
is there any wonder
when their capacity to absorb
reason and hypothesize
is limited to
'take your turn'
'stop here before going on'
'come to me for the answer'

What mind of - your own - can wonder
when automatically seeking an alternative
from monotony and assumption

Their own free higher will!
to explore and investigate
for growth - and contribution

To free our mind is to free the will of our Child-of-Light. It is a gradual dance of wonder and delight as we relearn the greater boundaries of our world. We open-to or align our energies with the greater expanse in higher dimensional consciousness, as we tap into the Universal force of truth and knowledge. Our 'child of light' within and also along with the third OverSoul in the Triad still in incubation to be born or completed here in the new Earth reality.

Lost My Focus
barraged by genuine need
all around me - theirs and mine
I still believe in basic need
originating in some past or time
we all need each other somehow
how far must I reach
to quell this need
from deep down under want
when does one replace the other
or do they just join forces in one quest

I do not know what I want anymore
because I do not need
any of those same objections
they have run their course again
here and now like so many
previous patterns encircling me
I just sit silently within - this whirlwind
and step into the show
when I am ready to take charge
and redirect mounting chaotic energies
into seeable solutions - in the 'now'
this momentary freedom
allowing just enough insight
to refocus from the void
creating a new gateway - with purpose
shifting - waiting - adjusting
and redirecting with new found focus

When One can still the mind to quell the bantering of preconceptions and endocrines, the OverSoul force shines out to rejuvenate and cleanse. Higher mindspace and OverHeart become One within us and in purpose to link to higher dimensions of consciousness. This interface exchange for inspiration of yin and yan combined experience and energizing focus. This the greater quest for upliftment - for new, higher unified focus with All; as we realign ourselves with conducive frequencies or vibrations of energy to filter into our world.

Father Figure

There isn't one other
so separate as you
always staying outside
with your position of control
there is no power there
yes you have built and built
and secured your reasoning
call it protection if you think we need that
but will you bind us all within your walls
as the foundation washes out with your death

Oh father, seed yourself
for all to feel your growth
your faith is your legacy
your old truths - not for us to judge
but we can carry you too
within these chambers
joining forces for the first time

The primal, masculine/feminine or twin-energies of each OverSoul, join forces in pairs for Earth's paradigm-shift to Triad higher dimensions of consciousness. Whereas the matriarch and the patriarch of our world and within each OverSoul have spent their feminine and masculine roles, through many lifetimes of timeline experience for the culmination of the joining in pairs through blending of both these energies/experiences; now the evolutionary time of the Kundalini for Lightbody development has been prepared. And We are carried through and with all OverChild bonds into the new dawn of the Triads' Light.

The foundation's washing out with the major masculine/yan old-reality death or collapse in consciousness. Probably nearly done and we are witnessing the push of remnant washouts now.

And the feminine/yin is still dealing with the old tendency to support issues, be the pacifier while the masculine/yan the old role of aggressor. This is changing as it has been the 'Feminine-Rising' in the last century especially that is of significance for this overall rebalancing at this point of major adjustments.

Wishing You

If I had shown you
you could have seen me better
but truths change in every healing moment
you can not help what you see
or can you? - help

In limiting ways
I have tried to reach out
wishing to see you beyond
but still I fall short
wishing only into my visions
and hopes for this world
but did you wish for my freedom
wishing to see more in me?
like I was wishing to see more in you
knowing these limitations encircling us
still wishing you - so much more
peace and contentment in your home
laughter which resounds
from every part of your being
echoing vibrations of bliss
out into this world
trusting that we will find
and feel our freedom!
seeing you always in a better light
and knowing you are of the same
family, visions, same future
unseen by all but carried by each
of our responsibilities

When we accept that our connection with our true match 'down here' only 'holds back' the issues as we will not treat each other in our usual ways of habitual tendencies to force a reversal of roles whenever the stagnation of codependance reach their limit, for otherwise we are bonded at the higher levels; we begin to believe in the sacredness and importance of what the Over connection is all about - pure love through the All - striving for growth in consciousness and upliftment for everyone in our lives.

Caregivers

Will you barter your child?
do you value their care
why - when there has never been
a place for them
shuffling them to the outskirts
of our society
and if they take our time
we do not thank them
but take it out on them
because they will take it
and take it
until we can see
time is not ours anyway
so do not trade them for it
only the illusion drains you
and only they truly care - for us

None of our space and time
in their world
but their need is our devotion
to the higher path
if they are to learn
to focus their attention
in a 'right' timely way
to channel their conducive energies
into this world
and contribute equally to Our best plan
showing us the nature of caring
for all things yet unseen

The sacredness of the Child lives through us and with us into future generations as we evolve and grow in consciousness becoming Triad Lightbody beings in physical reality. Our OverChild-of-Light plays the critical role of new example or true leader in mass-consciousness. We learn to take the steps necessary to focus our energy on always moving forward with trust and faith as any threatening collapse with ensuing washout naturally shifts relatively for All. We are initiated through dimensional shift-in-consciousness blending our composite parts as we become the Children of Lightbody consciousness.

Our OverChild or 'child of light' within along with the THIRD OverSoul in the Triad - all three still in incubation and to be born here simultaneously within new Earth reality. True matches are becoming or rebirthing each as an OverSoul as they finally truly join in pairs (by completing or linking all issues at a higher level for their respective lives) in partnered relationship in a new Triad community.

If I have come to trust in any one truth in this process, it is that we choose higher when we are gentle, patient and nurturing of our growth which is our healing. Patience is not waiting though - it is the wisdom to know what you need most.

I want less just when I begin to perceive the real need and then I usually continue to procrastinate and deny the true need but the process serves it purpose. We shed so many draining attachments (wants) in the physical this way. You can clean out your closets (issues) on every level and still the pulls or strings somewhat remain. Until we starve the intellect by stopping or consciously breaking/depriving habits, can we see the root of the problem (old conscious attachment). When we can no longer intellectualize why we need, want something or someone do we truly let-go - beliefs that are so firmly rooted in survival are truly lecherous to the Soul.

It is just that these concepts/beliefs, they are based on past experiences. It is so difficult to convey them in mere words - especially when understanding is in large part based on experience. If we could totally separate them - we would believe me. Someday I'm sure we'll be able to totally separate the understanding of these lessons/concepts from the actual events. (similar to any trauma really)

I truly believe that deeply rooted traumas eventually surface understanding when it is conducive. The traumas are serious stuff - from god knows how many lifetimes. We really won't need to 'resurface' when we stop the repeating of old lessons of experience and just go home (move on higher) without jumping through all the hoops; find understanding choosing higher ways.

Now I Begin

If I look at you closely enough
then I see what I do
nearly all of me
does not want to know this truth
that I look outside
or to other for a clue
of where to go next
of who to learn from now

Can't you see
you have always been my example
and I would never go that way
fight you until I run against every wall
and fall down once more
to make you feel my pain and truth
always easier for me to see your weakness

So father don't let me disappoint you anymore
because you can't do that for me either
your weaknesses are mine too
and so are your strengths
so let's not make fools of one another
stand up now and look around you
we have never been closer to each other
sense the humour of this life
a rich laughter full of irony and plunder
as we take from one another
and spoil with all this pain
just to feel the simplicity of our truth

I will not do that dance with you any longer
it tires me to the Core and reveals my aches
they can't endure the pain of rivalry
and I want my freedom now

Do you still believe
that there is more - beyond
what are we waiting for
maybe it will come for us
when we choose, just for this life

Going beyond the walls of preconception, beyond the places of origin in belief systems and patterns within karmic record is to link with the limitlessness of the Universal-force of the All-of-creation. We can rise above the rivalry of imbalance in our lives and tap into a greater awareness, allowing conducive frequencies to interweave with the rising force within - in turn blending our composite, dimensional energies. And where we once found our example in either father or mother, yin or yan expression at any given time in our Earth, we now look to completion with this new example or role with Our OverChild union - and with all OverSoul pairs' energies/ experiences for Triad completion. The twin, codependance of 'one or the other' roles are now finding an end with and through the Earth's yin and yan adjustments as we bring this divine creation-energy of the Creative-Source into everyday living.

There are so many times we would just rather stop - and we do, I mean completely stop all our notions (questioning everything we have ever wanted or needed even) especially during times of crisis. We just wonder if our life will ever settle. We find ourselves completely collapsed (everything washing out or coming to an end of sorts) and still comfortable with ourselves. This is our settled - temporary periods of settling for nothing at all to work out the way we planned. We can eventually accept that this collapse or ending to the way we have been approaching our life must have a time - a time period for renewal to begin again, like a huge readjustment.

Why must we continually go through many readjustments or collapses? Because the Earth is evolving so rapidly now (and we either keep pace or suffer profoundly) We realize eventually the less we fight or try to figure it out the more smoothly it goes (we feel more alive - we can feel through it all). And of course we come to learn and trust that there is always a huge miracle that awaits us afterward - so that everything we had planned or dreamt of - manifests so much better than what we could even imagine. My life is a testament to this.

Rise Above

If I asked you
would you grant me forgiveness
the wisdom to feel
where I have been stuck
and to understand this healing ache
lingering from so deep in some lifetime
yearning for redemption
acting itself out, time and again
seeking recognition of the truth
where I have dumped on others
and they in turn have dumped on me
their beliefs, their truths, their patterns
but not theirs - those from other times too!
and if I forgive - give and take back
am I redeemed?

Only when these limiting patterns stop!
how does it all stop
how do we heal
and not hold onto this ache
it acts out without warning sometimes
like a deep vengeance from the past or other time

These shadows suffocate
and dark spirits surmount my being
pushing me head crazy away from my fears
as this warrior fains
going to war with some past other time
by taking it into the future?
how do we stop and carry it no further
from here to another's burden
bringing all timeline debts to a clearing
taking responsibility for right now!

It all feels like too much
all these lifetimes of bad debt
on top of me like a depressing fate
pushing me back into my cocoon
waiting for a miracle

to transform me to a freer
avenue of expression
because I cannot act out
until I feel worthy and excited
enough to soar above
strong enough to be true
to all that ails in my world

I will not give back
and I cannot take back either
what I have done is too much more
than just me anymore
too much more than any - One
could feel or carry or heal

So carry me over
to my higher place of healing
for all it is I am and we are together
so much more than all this ache
where Our redeeming qualities together
will lift our hearts from these perilous times
above this earth's quagmire of re-enactments
to higher dimensions of consciousness
for multitudes of solutions
for our parts and Our role
in this grand awakening process

We are called to rise above karmic entrapment or predetermination by always choosing a higher path - even when we don't know exactly what that path may be in any moment in time - and when we only have our intuition and faith to go on. We might have since learned at least a million times over that this karmic reality is exactly the consciousness we are dealing with and need to rise above.

We can't TRY to perceive our true match. All we need is to just open and let the love surface within. And we recognize that - their presence - their love within. It's easy to feel that. We recognize this presence and have since we first crossed paths whether in the dreamstate, the meditative state or the physical.

Revelations

What then, to know the truth
but not to see it?
let's not revel in these times
illusions run deep and thick all around
while truth stays silently within
still with intent and clear focus
knowing the course and time
of an outward place

To seek truth is to feel it, to trust it
only acting on it's behalf
trusting your works, trusting their time
whether first or last
combined together lastly, most of all
their purposes far greater now
far reaching from there to here
working together to challenge and shift
our perspective and course of true action
while bridging realities

Yet truth still waits
while changing and growing
and adjusting within
no leap from there to here
just patience and nurture
while metamorphosis endures
travelling seven to twelve
weaving back and forth
a foundation is built for higher ground

Moving from the emotional flood waters
creating a bridge to that sacred place
with the comforter and cleanser
the Kundalini force
carrying with it the wrath of the beast
from the bottomless pit
to the scorching of the fire
the OverHeart Force

This sacred marriage of energy systems
carrying over of the old for the new
new world energy-system of One body
where Earth endures for all
Earth bears the truth of twelve
Earth the forerunner for all
and all sacrifice with her adjustments
to channel our energies forward
preparing all for the becoming
of the Children of We-consciousness

Whereas One split to become two separate OverSoul entities and twin relationship was born; now the two birth anew as they blend and combine with us for an Over-Oneness again, completing their mission for this Triad union. One OverSoul/Child entity is now born between us two as we both have adapted and expanded to fill our pair of OverSoul roles. We are Triad relationship newborn into a new Earth reality consciousness.

Triad relationship is coming for us - that means we will achieve the twin-Oneness of a third Combined OverSoul consciousness between our respective Triad partner's OverSoul consciousness and our own OverSoul consciousness. So that means One between Two to make Three. It just means a complete state of balance - no more leaning or even swaying or switching back and forth which is what all of humanity has always been struggling with alot. Not that humanity hasn't been able to achieve some semblance of balance at times in relationship between the yin and yan - its just that it is time for Earth to evolve from this 'battle for balance'.

The real crux with twin Lightbodies, together consciously to some degree, thereby sharing in the physical is that they need to stand as pillars or bonded OverSouls for both their sakes before the Combined Consciousness really can join/birth. The bond has been growing for several lifetimes but ultimately we have to trust in that Overbond with our flow of exchange for balance within ourselves for each other. We cannot 'battle for balance' and never could. Joining is and has always been a gradual bond of trust and Love continuing to build - like great pyramids.

Alphabetical List of Titles and First Lines

(Where the title is the same as the first line or few words)

'Inner Initiate'   (Acrylic, 16 ³/₄"h x 14"w)

Author Bio

From small rural community living in my youth, my love and respect for some greater order between all life forms on this planet was deeply set in my consciousness at a very early age. I had a natural, open trust while in nature and spent many hours comforted by its warmth and beauty. It seemed to feed or uplift my spirit so that I have learned to trust my innate understanding of this life force of prana around me, that is our own auric energy field exchanging with nature's force. And as Earth is going through a greater accelerated evolutionary change now, I simply have learned to trust in my own unfoldment as a part of all this. Whether we are being urged along by our own limitations or just along for the joy ride seems to be both part of the story. And I have learned to trust in a higher process of growth for All that is ours at the higher dimensions as well as down here with our changing Earth reality.

I learned an early avid fascination for diverse personalities with all the experiences of growing up in a large family of siblings and cousins along with small town neighbours. And since my late teens I have traveled for schooling and jobs often from city to city having lived in Ontario and also across Canada. I have settled in several countryside settings too and all the while meeting many wonderful and interesting people over the years. I have cherished many enough to call home and friend with fond and lasting memories, these many decades. And some of the best growth and learning came from these many early and later relationships, meetings and exchanges that cannot possibly be measured.

My most significant bond of inner relationship or OverSoul connection awakened within me to a greater degree when I reached a pivotal or critical point in my life of needing serious change. I began studies in several healing art modalities at this time in the mid 90's, when my choices for change stirred within me a desire to meet the challenge of a quickening inner unfoldment. I have worked mainly in the arts, mostly as a freelancer and focusing mostly on writing including poetry and songwriting these last 15 years or so. My choices for greater expression and joy have been the uplifting force in my life and while it can be unsettling at times to embrace the ever increasing and 'earth-shattering' Universal love/joy vibration that is raising consciousness or accelerating change everywhere in our world, it is also definitely fulfilling.

Author's Note

I wish to speak as plainly as is possible for the idea of greater community consciousness coming together for the future of Earth existence. If everything has brought us to this point of craving for so much more than we have ever known in this world - and maybe we could never really completely 'grasp' for a reason - because we simply were not at this point of dimensional consciousness converging or coming together for All at this time. If we are only now becoming more consciously responsible for the future - for technological advancement and greater moral decisions that affect our world, our galaxy and the cosmos so that accelerated conscious growth has a purpose now - to *carry* or move us on at a relative accelerated pace for what now is just too quick for us to 'latch onto' any specific movement or mentality or linear, conceptual-based ideology. Then I wonder, was new higher community really the point all along? This idea that all our karmic predetermined choices (regrettable ones to say the least) for this lifetime especially - were for greater good? If all of it was for this coming 'together consciously' at the higher levels for Earth's evolutionary shift, I guess we should be 'thanking lucky stars'.

If moving or evolving beyond the limitations of the karmic matrix was the point all along then we definitely arrived here in this lifetime with a heavy burden indeed. And shifting into lightbody awareness allowed us the greater insight to know or recognize when we could leave behind collapsing or evolving cyclical patterns to move higher consciously; ultimately breaking all karmic prechosen promises or all those old responsibilities or burdens of karmic accountability that were carried over from previous or other lifetime existences. In fact lightbody probably enabled us to carry those heaviest of burdens for at least a few lifetimes for all concerned for this time of our multidimensional greater awakening of abilities to move beyond the predetermination of karma and incorporate our 'overall' lessons at the higher levels. We witness and feel the resolutions of those obstacles which are just fate's cruel grip trying to hold us to other linear timeline world's of consciousness.

I think it is important that the inner child is coming into greater awareness in this time as abuse of the child is also brought into the light of day along with the growth in consciousness. For many generations that truth has slowly surfaced most especially in the last few decades now the experts declare children (both boys and girls with roughly similar statistics) suffer abuse including sexual, emotional, mental and physical abuse (including humiliating, demeaning, manipulating, harassing, threatening harmful language or behaviour, denial of affection or abandonment, affecting our very survival concepts) which includes every single child and grown to adult living. There are degrees of severity in everyone for any particular instance of pattern. But over lifetimes of experience (whether ever female or male human existence) I do believe we all carry an equal load coming into this time of lightbody awakening.

And each Soul also has an equal footing when stepping it up to the higher path where multidimensional growth brings all strengths into play for a greater good, which is a bigger picture involving an overall sharing at the higher levels. Each inner child learns to walk anew through and with healing or clearing of lifetime issues. Walking anew is one thing though and ultimately where exactly do we go to step-up and live in our birthright here? Vibrationally we are growing and going together on this Earth. At the higher levels of consciousness those who are awakening now to some greater degree of lightbody awareness have already begun 'their' higher choices for a common goal of togetherness for all down here with them in the physical plane of existence.

Triad community here in physical reality is still the illusive concept though at this point or stage in our evolution. Twin existence is all Earth has known and by 'twin' I mean both yin/yan energies in all lifeforms. Of course yin and yan is still the natural order of all things to come being in a constant equal flow of exchange or symbiance with final Triad completion or union - new relationship within the new paradigm of community consciousness. That is more than pairs awakening to their Overbond and joining in togetherness at the higher levels. It is pairs joining in new higher community consciousness here on Earth. Triad pairs becoming OverSelves with and through their new Third combined OverSoul Oneness, completing their union as it is to be born *here* and with other Triads in community. It is profound to say the least.

And what does this mean for the future? Mostly hope for a bright new human existence here on Earth. My own best hope is that it might *begin* to manifest at some new higher conscious way of life *here* within the next century or so. And *manifest* is the key word here as it relates to resolution of karmic issues and patterns between pairs. After that completion of all patterns any guess is fair game when it comes to the possibilities of what can be created or who (higher souls) can be born of these new relationships here in a higher physical reality of Triad community on Earth. 'The sky is the limit' and vibrationally or dimensionally, this may well be literal in this sense of things to come.

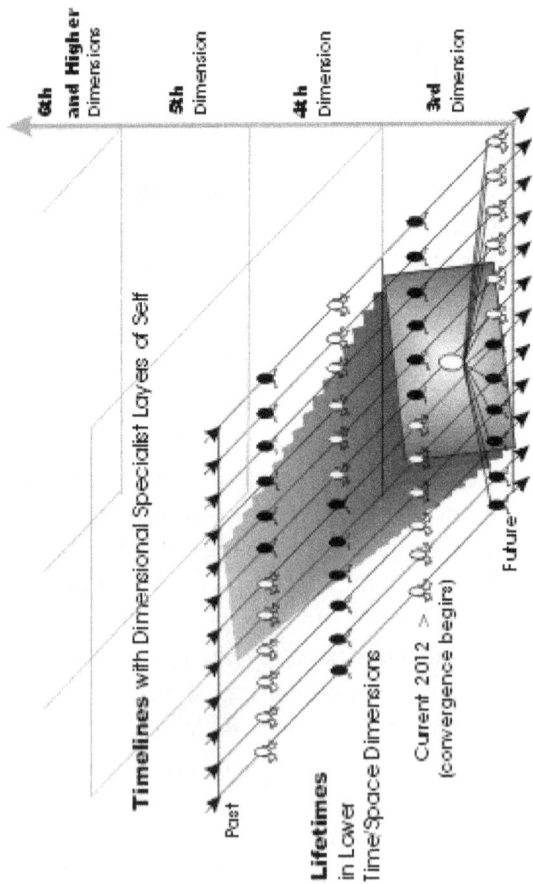

Timelines with Dimensional Specialist Layers of Self

6th and Higher Dimensions

5th Dimension

4th Dimension

3rd Dimension

Past

Lifetimes
in Lower
Time/Space Dimensions

Current 2012 >
(convergence begins)

Future

Astral Planes in 3rd Dimension

Female Lifetime

Male Lifetime

www.ingramcontent.com/pod-product-compliance
Lightning Source LLC
LaVergne TN
LVHW011204080426
835508LV00007B/589